Irmgard Wöhrl

THE **TRAPP** COOKBOOK

To my mother, Johanna Wiesinger

Irmgard Wöhrl

Imprint

The Trapp Cookbook is listed in the German National Bibliography; detailed bibliographic data can be viewed at http://dnb.d-nb.de.

© 2012 by Verlag Anton Pustet
5020 Salzburg, Bergstraße 12
Austria
All rights reserved.

Biography: Caroline Kleibel
English Translation: MB International Languages GmbH
Copy-editing: Fiona Schamberger
Proofreading: Martina Schneider
Cover: Tanja Kühnel
Production: Nadine Löbel
Printed by: Druckerei Theiss, St. Stefan im Lavanttal
Printed in Austria

Further informations: www.dastrappkochbuch.at

ISBN: 978-3-7025-0676-6

www.pustet.at

Image credits:

Cover: Stockfood
Page 7: Colorama Verlag Salzburg
Page 13, 19: Printed with the authorization of Unterach village hall
Page 70: Franz Wendl (Mondsee)
Page 10, 100: Wolfgang Weinhäupl (Mondsee)
Page 40: Reinhard Weidl (Berchtesgaden)
Page 104: Nadine Löbel
Photo of author Irmgard Wöhrl: Bettina Hana
Ambience photos: Tanja Kühnel
The historical images come from the private archives of the Leitner/Wiesinger/Wöhrl families.
All other pictures © Günther Pichlkostner (Vienna).

Irmgard Wöhrl

THE **TRAPP** COOKBOOK

Original Recipes from the Family Kitchen

VERLAG ANTON PUSTET

Index of Recipes

Content

25 jänner 2007

Mit Freude habe ich erfahren, daß Johanna Raudaschl, die 1931 bei unserer Familie Köchin war, wieder in unser Gedächtnis gerufen wird.

Ihre Enkelin, Irmgard Wöhrl, wird die Rezepte und Lebensgeschichte ihrer Großmutter und der Zeit, in der sie bei uns war, in einem Buch beschreiben.

Johanna Raudaschl war eine von Gott begnadete Köchin, die unseren Vater bei einem Festessen nach einer Jagd im Salz-kammergut so beeindruckt hat, daß er sie sofort zu uns nach Aigen bei Salzburg gerufen hat.

In Irmgard Wöhrls Buch werden Sie Episoden aus unserem Familienleben lesen, die noch nie veröffentlicht wurden: Die Familie Trapp durch die Augen unserer besten Köchin gesehen.

Ich bin ganz sicher, daß dieses Buch ein großer Erfolg werden wird und hoffe auf eine baldige Übersetzung in die englische Sprache. Mit besten Wünschen!

Maria von Trapp

Credential

I am delighted to hear that Johanna Raudaschl, who was the cook for our family in 1931, is to be remembered once again.

In this book her granddaughter, Irmgard Wöhrl, shares the recipes and tells her grandmother's life story including the time she spent with us.

Johanna Raudaschl was a divinely gifted cook who impressed our father so much at a banquet after a hunting trip in the Salzkammergut that he immediately invited her to become cook at our home in Aigen near Salzburg. Here you will read previously unpublished episodes from our family life: the Trapp family as seen through the eyes of our best cook.

I am certain that this book will be a great success.

With best wishes,
Maria von Trapp, Vermont in 2007

Maria von Trapp still has fond memories of the cook Johanna Raudaschl.

'With God begun, the day is won.'

Each of her recipe books written in kurrent script begins with this sentence as a dedication: *'Mit Gott begonnen, ist schon gewonnen.'* [With God begun, the day is won.]

My grandmother Johanna Raudaschl was a very devout woman. She grew up in a farming family, and religion influenced her life from early childhood. She was born out of wedlock in August 1904; this carried a stigma at that time in the small rural community in the Salzkammergut [a lake district in Upper Austria]. Because her mother, my great-grandmother, also had to go to work as a farmhand after the birth of her daughter, Johanna Raudaschl grew up under the strict care of her grandmother.

Never quite satisfied and yet never unhappy, she came to terms with her destiny. Diligent, strong and self-confident, she went her own way, which for a while – probably the most important time of her life, as she often said – led her to the home of the Trapp family. My grandmother cooked for the Baron, the Baroness, their children, and their guests. This was a very responsible position that called for acquired knowledge, as well as vigilance, interest, inventiveness, and imagination. Concerned with every-day essentials for those entrusted to her care, she never thought of herself. But the fact that she was able to prepare excellent meals even during meager times brought her appreciation and recognition, which provided her with an inexhaustible source of energy and courage to face life.

Despite the necessary respectful distance, an almost friendly relationship with mutual esteem quickly developed between Johanna Raudaschl, and her employer Baroness Maria Augusta von Trapp, who was exactly five months younger. When my grandmother later told me about her experiences in the Trapp family household, I always sensed a special harmony between the two very different women. I already loved these stories when I was a little girl. I was very close to my grandmother and could talk with her about everything.

She was a wonderful cook and I probably inherited some of her talent. When she passed away in 1993, aged 89, after a life both fulfilled and full of hardship, she left me her cookbooks. They were old, yellowed, and covered with all types of stains, and when I held them in my hands – almost like relics – various little pictures of saints, newspaper clippings, and notes fell out. A treasure trove! And so it has long been my wish not to let her life, her recipes, and her recipes for life, be forgotten. With great joy, I began to cook and sometimes had the feeling that my grandmother was standing next to me, helping me a little. Although she had written down the ingredients, there were rarely precise notes or instructions on how to cook the dishes step-by-step. After all, she had always done everything by instinct.

Against the background of Johanna Raudaschl's life story, it was important to me to make this book as authentic as possible and to capture both the spirit of the interwar period and the meal plan at the Trapp house. The cuisine presented here is simple and tasty. After all, what is truly good is timeless, even if tastes may change through time.

Remembering all the good things my grandmother prepared in the Trapp house, as well as her good deeds in life: 'With God.'

Irmgard Wöhrl

Author Irmgard Wöhrl and Roland Essl trying out Johanna Raudaschl's original recipes.

My humble self

A cool welcome in the hot summer of 1904

The touching and eventful life story of my grandmother Johanna Raudaschl began at the Holzberg farm, above the picturesque Lake Attersee around St. Bartholomew's Day (24 August), 1904.

That summer was unusually hot and dry until late August, which meant that the first hay harvest could take place earlier than in other years. It was a good one. Just as the meadows were noticeably threatening to dry up, the rain everyone had been longing for finally came at the end of August, bringing cool relief.

The farmer's daughter Theresia Raudaschl paid little attention to what was going on around her. She had very different worries as she set off on this mild, rainy August day on the arduous path that led from her parents' Holzberg [wood mountain] farm to her sister's, in order to bear her first child, under her sister's care. It was not exactly a joyfully awaited event, even though the baby came from the encounter with her first great love. In the autumn of the previous year, the 25-year-old, inexperienced Theresia met a migrant worker from the Salzburg area at a village fair and fell head over heels in love with him. But the secret meetings were not without consequences. They had even spoken of marriage, but then the man is said to have continued on his way to work in the quarry in Hallein. When Theresia realized that he had left her with a keepsake, she was quite despondent and stayed home with a broken heart. For a long time she did not risk admitting her condition. While her brothers Franz and Matthias showed

Johanna's mother
Theresia Raudaschl
(1878–1963).

little to no sympathy for the expectant mother – they were only concerned with her capacity for work, which gradually deteriorated under the emerging circumstances – Theresia found refuge with her sister Johanna.

Together with her husband, Johanna ran a small farm on the opposite shore, in Steinbach on Lake Attersee. In order to reach it, Theresia first had to hang a linen sheet from the balcony of the farmhouse on the Holzberg. This signaled to the ferryman below that someone wanted to cross the lake and he prepared for the journey. Then it took her a good hour to walk down the mountain to the landing place and reach the other shore with the boat. Two days later, on August 26, 1904, Theresia gave birth in Steinbach to a girl: 'My humble self,' as Johanna Raudaschl formulated it in her memoirs. And it was actually the more than dignified restraint or the modesty that was so typical for my grandmother throughout her life that allowed her to use this rather disdainful description of herself. A child born out of wedlock during this era was considered to be a 'mishap' and a considerable disgrace at that. But the most important thing appeared to be that the birth went well and mother and daughter were both in good health. The courageous aunt embraced her sister, toward whom

Theresia's sister Johanna (1882–1945) gave her support in the difficult time of the birth of her child.

she had always felt a tender bond of affection, and assured her that she was not the first and quite certainly not the last woman who would experience something like this.

How right she was. But nothing changed the fact that children born out of wedlock and their mothers were predominately treated as outsiders at that time. This was an appalling injustice and a circumstance that, it seemed to me, troubled my grandmother throughout her entire lifetime. In contrast to this supposed stigma, she had many positive experiences such as the affection of caring and especially understanding relatives who guided her destiny during the early years and gave her more stability than her mother could. It was probably a result of her personal experiences that Johanna developed a very distinct sense of justice and solidarity, which she maintained up to a ripe old

Johanna Raudaschl's birth house in Steinbach on Lake Attersee.

age. She was self-confident and assertive, clever, and humorous. And at some point she even attained the comforting certainty – without any haughtiness – that she had achieved something in her life despite all of the obstacles.

One of these understanding relatives who influenced her first days on earth was her aunt. And she was also the one who carried the newborn girl to Steinbach to be baptized the day after her birth and gave her the name of 'Johanna' as her godmother. 'Hannerl' is what she was called later. However, no one spoke much with the baby at the beginning because the aunt had to do her work and her mother only recovered gradually from the strain of the birth. She wanted to just stay in bed for the first week, but that was not possible. After a few days, she already had to go back home, across the lake, and up the Holzberg mountain. The harvest work was waiting and she had already been away for much too long. This did not suit her strict brothers at all because every hand was very important for the work back then. After all, there were no machines or other technical aids. Reaping had to be done with a sickle and scythe. There was a tremendous variety of work for the farmers to do on the farm and in the stables. Someone had to take care of the animals, the fields required full attention from the sowing to the harvest. In addition, every farmer was his own craftsman. And then there were also the forests of the Holzberg farm. Accord-

Unterach, Johanna Raudaschl's home village, on a postcard from the year 1907.

ing to the old saying, a farm without a forest is like a bed without a cover. The name Holzberg (wood mountain) farm did not refer – as could have been presumed – to a special abundance of woodlands but just to the location near the forest. Still, the family owned the 10 to 15 hectares customary for the region and there was constantly work to be done.

Work was not just a part of life, but a necessity and its foundation. It belonged to life like the seasons, like the sun and rain. So the brothers preferred to accept the disgrace of the unmarried birth instead of sending the sister away and losing an important farmhand. The little daughter was simply wrapped in a blanket and taken along to the field. It was a truly cool welcome.

Strict but warm-hearted

Johanna's youth with her grandmother

Theresia's mother, whose name was also Johanna, was 53 years old when her granddaughter was born. She was a resolute woman who ruled the farmhouse with a firm hand, while the grandfather diligently did his day's work, cultivated the fields together with his two sons, herded the livestock, and sometimes smoked a pipe as he relaxed in the evening sun on the bench in front of the house. Although she was initially not enthused about her daughter's illegitimate offspring, little Johanna soon succeeded – in a way that only children manage – in touching the heart of her reluctant grandmother. Was it because of the mutual first name, which was already a family tradition? Was it because of Hannerl's sunny nature? In any case, the grandmother soon kept the little girl with her in the house while the mother went off to work. Before long, she also helped out at other farms in the region in order to earn her livelihood.

Johanna grew up in a rural world that has long become foreign to us today. Far removed from any romanticism of the 'good old days', her first years were already characterized by meager circumstances with many hardships and hard work. However, they were also shaped by strong gratitude toward seemingly little things, as she often recounted, as well as piety and a zest for life. People resigned themselves to the inevitable and calmly accepted 'that the wind blew through drafty windows and on winter mornings the bedspread was white with snow.' Because the housing conditions were so cramped, Johanna was allowed to sleep in her grandmother's bed. It is touching to read that she could even make a virtue out of this lack of space when she shared her memories of how: 'I warmed her back and she warmed my feet, which were always cold. So we were well suited'

The year 1911 was dry but productive. On August 24th, there was a devastating storm that uprooted entire forest stretches in the area, as well as ripping out many fruit trees, taking roofs off houses, and causing major damage. The Holzberg farm was thankfully spared for the most part, which the grandparents saw as a good omen. In keeping with the family tradition, that same year they handed down the farm to their firstborn, Johanna's uncle Franz. Together with their seven-year-old granddaughter, the old couple moved to the room set aside for their retirement at the left front corner of the farmhouse. It had a wonderful view across the lake.

Of course, Johanna had little time to look at the splendid panorama because she already had to lend a helping hand at an early age. Games or festivities rarely interrupted her chores and duties. She had to herd the livestock in the pastures around the nearby Lake Egelsee and make sure that none of the animals got stuck in the marsh. She spent the entire day outdoors. Johanna was afraid of the snakes sunning themselves everywhere, hidden in the grass. An adder's bite was no joke and the doctor was far away. Even as a little girl, she was already very proud when the livestock was in good shape and clean and when each cow had safely found its way back to the stall in the evening. Then she had to mow the meadows and turn the hay and make sheaves out of the grain: 'Good exercise for the back! By the evening, you knew what you had done during the day.' In order to store the hay in the barn, it had to be stamped, a boring, repetitive process during which there was a lot of dust. The entire body itched and prickled. The only ray of hope was the prospect of being allowed to jump from the very top into the hay with a 'yippee' when the job was done. Picking potatoes and digging the mangold, the so-called mangelwurzels, out of the earth seemed to Johanna like a rather hunchbacked occupation. Her witty comment was: 'It's a good thing I wasn't not so tall because it wasn't as far to the ground.'

The work in the house was also never-ending. The chores expected of Johanna as a child were not just minor ones. She was responsible for essential housekeeping tasks, such as strenuously scrubbing the old wooden floor. If people didn't bring enough dirt into the front room, the chickens did the job. Because they were so important for the food supply back then, they were kept in the house during the cold season and had their coop under the bench. Yet, everything still had to be scrubbed clean. 'And Grandmother', as Johanna wrote in her memoirs, 'who was already somewhat sickly at that time, would watch me as I worked to make sure I did everything right. If she wasn't satisfied with what I did, she would immediately shake her index finger threateningly in the air. Then I knew something was wrong and had to work even harder. Grandmother was very strict but today I know that her strictness was for my own good and it never would have occurred to me to contradict her.'

Beginning in May 1911, Johanna Raudaschl attended the Catholic elementary school in Unterach on Lake Attersee. At that time it was considered a privilege for a child to be permitted to go to school and several children from each of the different grades shared the same classroom. The strenuous path that she had to take in both summer and winter, rain or snow, sometimes even before the break of day, was almost four miles long. During the summer, she was required to already be at church at seven a.m. for school mass. First she had to walk down the mountain and then along the lake. In winter, Johanna had a hard time with the long skirts that proved to be especially impractical when trudging through knee-high snow. But pants for girls? That was unheard of and inconceivable. It simply was not a possibility and Johanna certainly had no desire to be the first to risk creating such a fashion. How could she have? Even the skirts that she wore were used or sewed from remnants. Her grandmother was skilled and showed her how to make something useful out of every last bit. The long evenings were reserved for handiwork. They spun the flax, wove, knit, and embroidered, and while the hands were at work, the thoughts were free to roam. The little dress that her grandmother sewed for her long-awaited first communion turned out especially beautiful. Johanna felt like a little princess in it. Nothing was thrown away, everything was recycled, and they obviously took good care of what they had. 'Take care of your heart' was the saying embroidered in red yarn on a linen pillow that made the simple room look a bit homier. Johanna decided at

The eight-year-old Johanna at her first communion in the summer of 1912.

a very young age to take this saying to heart.

She often arrived at school frozen stiff on winter days and was permitted – because she was such a diligent student – to sit near the warm tiled stove. The icicles on the hem of her skirt gradually began to melt and the rough sheep's wool socks started thawing. This was indescribably itchy, but at least her clothes were dry before she set out on the way home again. She was not only responsible for herself, but also always had to accompany a horde of neighbor's children on the way down to Unterach and back again. Everyone knew that they could depend on Hannerl. So she once had to take along to the village a broken window that needed new glass. Another time it was a broken pot that had to go to the metalworker and be carried back up the mountain again a few days later. On top of this, she was hungry. During the week, it was usually just sour soup and potatoes that awaited her at home. So it was no wonder that one day, when Johanna's grandmother had once again sent her to Unterach to buy some yeast and other things, the girl suddenly felt famished on

The Holzberg farm around 1922. Theresia Raudaschl, her brother Franz, and Johanna's little half-brother Max.

However, Johanna Raudaschl did not forget to mention in her diary entries that the winter also had its good sides and that life did not just consist of toil and trouble: 'The winter,' she once wrote, 'was almost my favorite time, especially when we went to get wood up in the forest. When there was a good toboggan run, the entire village turned out to ride the firewood. This was a lot of fun and the ringing of the horse bells could be heard from far away. Once the wood was loaded, everyone rode down the mountain. This was really wild. I was afraid the first time and decided to just run behind it, but later I also sat on it'.

Some aspects of their everyday lives changed when the First World War broke out in the summer of 1914. It was not for the better. Both uncles, who had worked on the farm, were required overnight to enlist in the army. The grandfather, who had already retired from active life on the farm and only helped out in exceptional circumstances, now had to do the heavy work in the fields once again. The old man began to sharpen his scythe and mow the grass at 4 a.m. Of course Johanna had to help as well. Before she went to school to learn writing and arithmetic, she had already raked the fields.

'I finished elementary school in 1918. Senior teacher Ms. Hölzl filled out the best graduation diploma, which I can still show anyone today,' grandmother later noted in her diary, not without pride.

On the other hand, the family high up on the Holzberg did not hear too much about the

the way home. No-one will miss a little crumb of the yeast, she thought, and broke off a piece. It didn't taste good, but it was satisfying and it inevitably turned into more than just one bite. This was followed by another and then another. The otherwise very conscientious girl irresponsibly ate the yeast and arrived home with empty hands. Whether the grandmother's finger just circled threateningly in the air or whether there was a more severe punishment for this offence was never revealed in the story …

major upheavals related to international politics. Although they knew that Austria was only left with a very small portion of the former Austrian-Hungarian monarchy after the war and the young state was therefore faced with great economic problems, the people on the Holzberg were largely spared the difficulties during the post-war years – famine, lack of coal, inflation, and unemployment. It was a good thing that all of them were so undemanding at that time. The sour soup, the cabbage, and the potatoes from their own field were also there in difficult times, so at least none of them had to go hungry. There was inflation after the war, in which the prices were fifteen times higher than in 1914. Johanna Raudaschl's grandparents and mother lost almost all of their savings. The little bit they had turned into nothing so that the grandfather couldn't even buy tobacco for his pipe. The 'tobacco' that he grew himself did not agree with him. He soon died of lung disease. In 1919, Johanna's mother bore a second child out of wedlock when she was already 41 years old. Johanna suddenly had a little brother. How close joy and suffering can sometimes be: On March 2, 1920, her beloved grandmother died and Johanna wrote in her diary: 'For me the sun went down.'

Unterach 1926. The Raudaschl family's Holzberg farm also offered such a breathtaking view of Lake Attersee and the Höllengebirge [mountain range].

3 1/3 cups (800 ml)	water
1 cup (250 ml)	sour cream
3 1/2 tbsp (25 g)	flour
1	garlic clove
4	juniper berries
15	peppercorns
1	bay leaf
1 tbsp	caraway seeds
1 tsp (7 g)	salt
1 tsp (7 g)	bouillon mix
1	shot of vinegar

Sour Cream Soup

Bring water to boil with the garlic clove, juniper berries, peppercorns, bay leaf, and caraway seeds and simmer for about 30 minutes. Stir sour cream until smooth with some water and flour and mix into the seasoned water. Add the salt, bouillon mix, and vinegar. Bring to a boil again. Strain through a sieve and season to taste.

Serve with boiled potatoes, diced ham, or pumpernickel croutons.

Sour cream soup is a simple dish that was often served in earlier times. It was inexpensive and tasty.

Delicious roast, woman's boast

Culinary childhood memories

Her steady hand almost appeared to stroke the meat selected for roasting. With precise motions, she skillfully chopped the dewy garden herbs – a fragrant addition to a precious piece of roast. Everything was expertly arranged in a polished pan. Even in its raw state, the work was a credit to its creator. 'Meat,' my grandmother always used to say, 'is something very special.' She had had to live without it for too long in her childhood and youth. Meat dishes tended to be the exception at the beginning of the 20th Century and only served on the farmhouse table for holidays. Even then, it usually wasn't young, tender poultry that landed in the pot but 'the tough old boiling fowl that had to be cooked for ages.'

It was always a special joy for me to watch my grandmother work in the kitchen. I learned a great many things from her – just like she herself had inherited the love of cooking from her grandmother.

Wilhelm Busch once wrote: 'Good deeds may fittingly include the preparation of fine food', and later: 'A savory, delicious roast, can only be a woman's boast.' He must have known

Johanna Raudaschl. With her passion for cooking, no ingredient was too insignificant and no detail too unimportant. Even when she lived with her grandparents, in the room set aside for their retirement up on the Holzberg, Johanna's most delightful time was spent helping her grandmother with the cooking and baking. She loved the desserts more than anything else, but sugar was hard to get, rationed during the war, and the law even prohibited the 'making of cookies' at times. When there was cake for once, for a special occasion, even just the baking itself was the greatest joy. This enthusiastic willingness to help was not only based on the chance to lick the mixing spoon or stick her fingers into the batter – even though this certainly was one of the reasons. She also liked to carry out the more 'tedious' chores like sifting the flour, grating the nuts, and carrying wood or water – and stirring for hours. Just beating the egg white until it was properly stiff was strenuous and then there was the heavy batter. The egg yolks, sugar, and flour had to be beaten for an hour, always in the same direction. This is how her grandmother had instructed that it be done and Hannerl – usually – also did exactly what was asked of her. Just once she was overcome by curiosity and changed the direction for a few whisks. What now? Was the batter ruined? Would the cake collapse? Almost as soon as she had risked the prank, she was plagued by a bad conscience. When the hour was over and her grandmother poured the batter into the cake tin and put it in the oven, Johanna could no longer stand it in the small room. She didn't even want to lick the bowl anymore. She ran out and tried to distract herself with all kinds of games to avoid thinking about how there would inevitably be hell to pay when her grandmother found out. How could she have let herself get carried away like that? Her grandmother was already calling for her and she trotted back with her head hanging. But when she looked through the window into the room, she saw how her grandmother proudly looked at the gugelhupf [bundt cake] on the table that had risen higher than almost ever before – and when she saw Hannerl, she praised her with the words: 'See, it's because you stirred it so nicely.'

I can only guess what inner conclusions my grandmother, who was certainly very relieved, drew from this story at the time. What I noticed about her recipes time and again was: although she neatly listed all of the ingredients, she gave very little instruction regarding the actual preparation of the dishes. Was it this early-childhood experience from back then that allowed her to trust her own intuition after that? In any case, she did not want to put constraints such as exact stirring times, number of whisks, or instructions for the direction of the cooking spoon on herself or others who would cook according to her instructions. There was something else that was clear to Hannerl at an early age. She wanted to be able to cook as well as her grandmother – maybe even better, had this thought not seemed too haughty to her. When singing G'stanzl [Alpine sung verse] – singing was another one of Johanna Raudaschl's passions – one line became etched in her mind that she never wanted to be said of herself: 'The lassie got married at just seventeen, can't even cook porridge, she's really too green.'

After Martinmas at the beginning of November, when all of the outside work had been completed, it was slaughtering time during my grandmother's childhood. The family was always very happy when there was enough meat and some of it could be kept for their own needs. It was even better when it became cold and froze so that the delicacies stayed fresh for a long time. In order for the meat to be well aged, it was layered in a wooden tub and covered with much salt and garlic. The fat was melted and poured into clay pots, with the crispy greaves collecting at the bottom. One portion of the meat was hung on a fork in the fireplace for smoking, so that it lasted until spring when used sparingly because – except for the pig slaughter festivity – it was served only on Sundays and holidays. The slaughter was really a time of celebration. Various spices, salt, garlic, and onions were prepared days in advance. On the slaughter day itself, giant cooking pots were heated with water on the stove in the early morning. Johanna was not present when the animals' throats were slit.

The men did this: the grandfather, the uncles, and the neighbors who were glad to help out for a piece of pork. After the work was done – and this could take days – the cooked pork with cabbage and dumplings was served to the helpers as a present. It was a more than welcome change from the perpetual cabbage soup and potatoes.

Before each meal, the family stood together around the table and said the Lord's Prayer or a Hail Mary. The countless repetitions of grace had long turned the original text into an incomprehensible sequence of sounds that only the older generation understood. The younger people murmured along with them for the sake of decency, and recognized only the closing 'Fathersonandholyghostamen,' which was said while they made the sign of the cross on forehead, mouth, and chest. It was the sign that they were all finally permitted to begin eating. Everyone immediately reached for the jacket potatoes accompanied by thin little slices of bread that they soaked in the soup. The sour soup was served on mornings and evenings, before and after work in the stall. So when someone said 'Soup time,' everyone knew what was meant. Even breakfast was basically a 'soup meal' and that's what it was called. Whatever else was on the table beside the potatoes and soup depended on the imagination of the cook and the available food supply. Even if the variety was very meager, they never forgot to make the sign of the cross and say a courteous 'Thanks be to God' after the meal.

The Lord's Prayer says: 'Give us this day our daily bread.' This shows that the daily bread was not only far more important than today, but also how much more effort it took to make. Bread was considered to be a gift from God and it was greatly valued. Even the crumbs were never thrown away but used to feed the animals. They baked the loaves – rye bread or wheat-rye bread – themselves and there were all types of myths about them. Before cutting the bread, they made the sign of the cross above each loaf and had sayings like: 'Cut the slices fair and wealth shall be your share.' But if someone was not able to cut a loaf into equally thick slices, people said that he had already lied that day … Johanna Raudaschl wrote down an anecdote about this: 'If the blade of the knife was sharpened on just one side, the result could be that the pieces had varying thickness when the bread was cut. So when the slices of bread became thinner and thinner, people said that the farmer had sharpened the knife today. On the other hand, if the bread slices became thicker, the farmhand was probably involved.'

Baking bread was one of the focal points for life on the farm. Freshly baked bread with butter and salt was a coveted delicacy that was served very sparingly. Baking day was every two weeks. It was the women's task to stir the dough in a large trough in the kitchen the previous evening. In the early morning, the oven mortared in under the stove was heated with dry logs. After the wood ashes were swept out, they began sliding the loaves into the hot oven. The mouthwatering aroma of the fresh bread gradually began to spread throughout the entire house. In order to keep the appetite under control, the so-called Aschenzelten were made. These were oval flatbreads about the size of the palm of one's hand, similar to little pizza bases, which were formed from a reserved portion of the dough and placed in the oven after the loaves had baked. Because of the low heat, the flatbreads stayed half-baked and had a hard crust. Fresh out of the oven with salt and butter that slowly melted in the hollow of the flatbread, they were a real treat and stayed indelibly imprinted in childhood memories.

As the weekend approached, the cream – which Johanna's grandmother had skimmed from the milk into brown earthenware jars throughout the entire week – was whipped into butter. For Hannerl, these jars were a persistent source of bad conscience – especially when she was home alone and her stomach slowly began to rumble. Whether she wanted or not, her thoughts revolved incessantly around the thick layer of cream. It was hard to imagine what would have happened if everyone in the house had taken a few spoons of it!

At that time, the butter was still made by churning it by hand in a butter churn. After about half an hour, the butter separated from the buttermilk. The fat curdled into little lumps, which Johanna strained through a clean linen towel and then skillfully formed into a block of butter, which she was sometimes even allowed to decorate. The family liked to drink the remaining buttermilk, which was permitted but sometimes could excessively stimulate the digestion …

The major portion of the butter, made with such great effort, was sold and only a little was left for the family. This probably explains how good the buttered bread tasted, that she received as a reward after the work was done. Looking back, my grandmother's memories were often tinged with the magic of contentment and the undemanding happiness of childhood, which cannot be compared with anything else in the world and perhaps justified the attribute of 'good' for the 'old days'.

Reminiscing about her childhood, Johanna Raudaschl wrote: 'I was never really ill.' Her grandmother's dried blueberries helped against stomach-aches caused by buttermilk, apples that were too green, or unripe plums. Arnica was used to disinfect abrasions. Vinegar compresses were applied to calm fever. There were also time-tested household remedies for coughs and sore throats in winter, such as throat compresses of lard and onions, but they were hard to endure. Less smelly were the hot linden-blossom tea with honey or the delicious fir-tree syrup that caused Johanna to cough harder than was actually necessary. To make the cough syrup, the fresh tops were broken off the fir trees in May, layered in a large jar, and sweetened. Then the jars were left standing on a sunny windowsill for a few weeks, until a syrup formed, which was then bottled and given by the spoonful when necessary. People often say that the more effective the medicine is, the worse the taste. Fortunately, the fir-tree syrup that has proved effective through the decades does not follow this principle. It had the wonderful taste of the forest and still helped. Or was this a case of the solid faith that could move mountains?

Stewed elderberries with plums

Strip elderberries from umbels. Bring water to a boil with sugar, cinnamon stick, cloves, honey, and lemon juice. Then remove the spices. Add elderberries and plums and simmer until the plums are soft.

To create a creamy consistency, blend cornstarch with rum and add to the stewed elderberries.

This is a good side dish for typical Austrian desserts such as the Salzburger Nockerl and any kind of cream cheese pastries.

Tip: you can add a little grated apple or pear to refine the flavor.

3 1/3 cups (500 g)	elderberries
1/2 cup (100 g)	granulated sugar
4 tbsp	honey
1	cinnamon stick
5	cloves
	juice of 1/2 lemon
1/2 cup (125 ml)	water
1/2 lb (250 g)	plums, halved and pitted
Approx.1 tbsp	cornstarch
2 1/2 tbsp (4 cl)	rum

Liver pâté

1/4 lb (125 g)	pork liver
1/4 lb (125 g)	calf's liver
1 tbsp	butter
1/2 lb (250 g)	raw bacon, cut into cubes
1 tsp (5 g)	salt
1 1/2 tbsp (12 g)	cornstarch
1/2 tsp (1 g)	powdered sugar
1 pinch of	sodium nitrate
	pepper
	nutmeg, ground
	some slices of smoked white bacon, thinly sliced to line the pâté form

Heat butter and then brown the diced pork and calf's liver, as well as the raw bacon, for about 1 minute. Next, mince the mixture and blend well with the rest of the ingredients adding a little bit of water.

Line pâté pan with plastic wrap, cover with thinly cut bacon slices and fill with the mixture. Wrap the pâté in the bacon slices and close the plastic wrap. Simmer in a hot bain-marie in the preheated oven at 250°F (120°C) for about 1 hour. Let pâté cool, put in a cold place, remove from the pan, and cut into slices that are about 1/3 inch thick. Serve with stewed cranberries or Cumberland sauce.

The pâté can also be filled into little preserving jars and simmered in the bain-marie in the same way. It can be used as sandwich spread and will stay fresh for a few days in the refrigerator.

Rolled roast tenderloin

Sprinkle roast sirloin on one side with a mixture of bacon, bread crumbs, anchovies, marjoram, and ginger. Roll up meat and tie kitchen yarn around it.

Season the meat with salt and pepper.

Heat butter in a roasting pan and brown roast sirloin well on all sides, add the broth and simmer at 350°F (180°C) for about 20 minutes in preheated oven. Remove meat and undo kitchen yarn. Dissolve cornstarch in 3 tbsp of cold beef broth and thicken the sauce in the roasting pan with it. Finally, refine the texture of the sauce with whipping cream. Place the roast sirloin back in the roasting pan and let it rest for a few more minutes in the oven, which should be turned off.

Take the meat out, cut into slices, arrange, and cover with sauce. Serve with noodles, spaetzle, or Bohemian dumplings.

1 3/4 lb (800 g)	roast tenderloin of pork, cleaned, cut length wise and pounded (ask the butcher to prepare it this way)
1/4 lb (100 g)	streaky bacon, diced finely
2 tbsp	bread crumbs
1 tbsp	anchovies (in oil), diced
1 tbsp	marjoram, chopped
1 tbsp	ginger, very finely chopped
1 cup (250 ml)	beef broth (set aside 3 tbsp of cold beef broth for the sauce)
2 tbsp	butter
2 tbsp	corn starch
3 tbsp	whipping cream salt, pepper

Walnut-bread and 'Aschenzelten' [flatbreads]

Sponge:

3/4 cup (100g)	wheat flour
2 tsp	powdered sugar
1 1/2 tbsp (24g)	fresh yeast or 1 tbsp (8g) yeast, active dry

Dough:

3 1/3 cup (300g)	rye flour
2 3/4 cup (360g)	wheat flour (type 1050)
1/2 cup (100g)	natural sour dough starter
1 1/2–1 2/3 cup	milk water, lukewarm (1/2 milk, 1/2 water)
2 tsp	salt
2 tsp	bread spices (fennel seeds, coriander seeds, caraway, and anise)
2 tsp	honey
1 tbsp	sunflower oil
3/5 cup (80g)	tree nuts (may be mixed with shelled sunflower seeds)

Instead of tree nuts, other ingredients such as flaxseeds, sesame seeds, pumpkin seeds, or even bacon cubes can be added. Knead the selected ingredients into each portion of the dough.

First make the sponge by mixing the yeast, powdered sugar, and 3/4 cup (100g) of wheat flour, as well as about 1/3 of the milk water, into a thick paste. Cover this and let it rise in a warm place (for about 20–30 minutes) until it doubles in volume. Then add all of the ingredients and knead into a smooth dough (adding the milk water to achieve the right consistency). Dust the loaf with flour and let it rise in a warm place for about 30 minutes. Divide the dough into two parts, knead each part, form loaves, and let them rise again for another 30 minutes. Dust bread loaves with flour, place on a cookie sheet with parchment paper, and bake in the preheated oven at 430°F (220°C) on the middle rack for about 15 minutes. Then reduce the heat to 350°F (180°C) degrees and continue to bake for about another 30 minutes. For a nice crust, place a bowl with water into the oven during the first half of the baking time.

Aschenzelten:

Use some of the nut-bread dough and divide it into 1/2-cup (100g) portions on a floured work surface. Form into balls, press flat, and pull to make palm-sized ovals thin in the middle and thicker at the edges. Place on a lined cookie sheet and bake in a preheated oven at 430°F (220°C) for about 15–20 minutes. Then brush hot with melted butter and salt lightly.

2/3 cup (160g)	butter
4	eggs (two of them separated)
3/4 cup (100g)	powdered sugar
2 1/4 cup (200g)	pastry flour
1/3–1/2 (70–90 ml) cup milk	
1	pinch of salt
2 1/3 cup (200g)	almonds, peeled and ground
1 cup (100g)	almonds, sliced
5 tsp (16g)	baking powder
2 tsp (8g)	vanilla sugar
	zest of 1/2 lemon

This gugelhupf also tastes exquisite when three tablespoons of raisins are mixed in with the ground almonds!

Gourmet Gugelhupf [bundt cake]

Mix together flour and baking powder, sugar, and vanilla sugar. Beat soft butter very well with the mixer or food processor and add lemon zest, 1 whole egg, 2 tbsp flour, and 2 tbsp sugar.

Then continue to stir well. Add another whole egg, 2 tbsp flour, and 2 tbsp sugar. Next, add 2 egg yolks, flour, and sugar and continue to stir. In between, add the milk in spoonfuls, depending on the consistency of the batter. Repeat this process until all of the ingredients have been used. Then stir in the ground almonds. Finally, beat two egg whites with a pinch of salt and fold into the mixture.

Spread butter inside the gugelhupf form and line with almond slices. Scrape the batter into the form and bake in a preheated oven at 330°F (165°C) for about 50–60 minutes.

Apprenticeship years

Johanna's first position in Nussdorf

Toward the end of the last school year in 1918, around Whitsunday, Johanna's highly respected teacher Ms. Hölzl asked the girl to see her after class. Because this was so unexpected, Johanna was afraid that something was wrong. This was an unfounded fear because she had always been one of the best and most attentive students. And this is precisely what Ms. Hölzl was interested in because she wanted to know what Johanna planned to do after leaving school. Johanna explained that she wanted to stay at her grandparent's Holzberg farm, and then later perhaps work somewhere as a farmhand like her mother or, better yet, as a kitchen help. 'Wouldn't you prefer to learn a profession?' Johanna gave her teacher a sad and serious look. How would that be possible? Of course, it was her greatest desire to learn to be a cook, but her family was not able to pay for the training. After all, accepting an apprenticeship somewhere meant paying fees and where would she get the money? The grandparents were poor and her mother also had to pinch every penny. Furthermore, her visits had been rather few and far between over the years.

'Well, a self-confident girl like you will make her way in any case. Good fortune smiles on you!' Ms. Hölzl said and looked at the student for a long time before she dismissed her.

The last school day – and the last walk to school – came more quickly than she could have imagined. This would be her last summer on the Holzberg. Her grandmother, who probably already knew that she would not live much longer, had been able to set aside some money from the sale of crops and other food. She was also concerned with Hannerl 'finding a good position'. Even Johanna's mother Theresia wanted to contribute to her daughter's training: 'I would like her to have a better life'. So an apprenticeship as a cook at the Wiesinger – a reputable restaurant with a butcher shop attached – in Nussdorf on Lake Attersee – was found for Johanna through her relatives. So in the autumn of 1918, just after her 14th birthday, my grandmother, torn between joyful expectation and the melancholy of having to leave the Holzberg, packed her few belongings in a wooden suitcase and moved to Nussdorf.

She was very homesick during the first weeks and used every free day to go back to

Unterach. After her grandmother died in 1920 and – as she so touchingly wrote – 'the sun went down' for her – for a long time her grief prevented her from visiting the Holzberg farm. The scene of her childhood now appeared soulless and empty to her. Yet, as the saying so aptly puts it, 'whenever God closes a door, he opens a window somewhere else'. In the following years, Johanna preferred to stay down in Nussdorf and gradually enjoyed spending more of her scarce free time at her place of work. She met people and made friends. And even if the 'Golden Twenties', as they were often called, had a different meaning for people in the city, Johanna's life also shared a bit of the glamour. New clubs were formed that had a lasting influence on life in the village and, above all, attracted young people. Despite the hard work, Johanna discovered modest pleasures for the first time, went out, participated in the village fairs and folk dancing, and sang in the church choir.

In contrast to the solitary life up on the mountain, there were times when things were really happening here – at least under the circumstances at that time … 'I like to remember how things used to be in Nussdorf', Johanna wrote later. 'There were hardly any cars driving through the village. Only horses and rack wagons or bullock carts were on the road. But sometimes they also ran very fast or even bolted. Yet someone was usually able to catch the animals before something was broken or a real accident occurred.' The entire year was characterized by the traditional holidays and seasonal customs which reflected the rhythm of country life. There were church festivals such as the Corpus Christi processions or Thanksgiving and the farmers' holidays outside the harvest season. On Epiphany, the 'Gloeckler' went from house to house – these were children who, after they had sung the 'Gloeckler song', would be given 'Gloeckler donuts' by the farmers. This wandering horde was not dressed in any special way and had nothing in common with the Gloeckler of the inner Salzkammergut with their splendidly decorated headgear. Some of the farmers in Nussdorf were more generous and some more tight-fisted. Even today, people still talk about the crude pranks that threatened a farmer who gave them little or nothing …

On Candlemas (2 February), after which the days began to get perceptibly longer, farmers had to 'keep on' the servants that they needed in the following year on the farm, i.e. asked them to stay. All those who were not 'kept on' quietly left the farm in order to ask for work from another employer.

Both young and old met during the year in Nussdorf at the Wiesinger. The popular village inn was the local communication center and information exchange. The first summer guests – 'the gentlefolks' – soon arrived at Lake Attersee from Linz, Vienna, and later from Germany. They came with children, grandparents, and maids and – as Johanna Raudaschl remembers – 'they usually stayed for two months'. It was still a quiet form of tourism. The swimwear was very romantic: 'The ladies' swimsuits had ruffles round the high neck-lines and long sleeves and the pants were long and wide and went down to below the knees, where they were gathered with lace and frills. When the sun was shining, they all wore straw hats.' If their outfits seemed somewhat strange to the country girl Johanna, the customs of the distinguished summer guests seemed even more so. While flushing toilets were already standard in the better houses of Vienna, they were still completely unknown to the residents of Nussdorf; but since the Wiesinger inn-keeper did not want to be considered a coun-try bumpkin, he installed in the attic a water container which, when a summer guest pulled the 'handle', emptied through a drainpipe. The

illusion was perfect, but the water for the refill unfortunately always had to be lugged upstairs in buckets. This was a highly responsible task, with which the Wiesinger innkeeper naturally entrusted his Hannerl.

The locals and the summer guests collabor-ated in organizing some of the big summer fes-tivities. Among the 'gentlefolks' were generous benefactors such as Baron Eugen von Ransonnet and the opera diva Maria Jeritza. Thanks to the beauty of the landscape and the hospitality of the people, Lake Attersee offered many sources of inspiration – to the likes of the artist Gustav Klimt who often spent his summers in the region until the year 1916.

Off to new shores

Salzkammergut delicacies as a dowry

A welcome guest at the Wiesinger was Matthias Engljähringer, who was also an innkeeper and butcher from Strobl on Lake Wolfgangsee. He often visited to compare notes. When he once asked Johanna whether she would like to come and cook for him, she didn't have to think twice about the answer. She had no family that she was especially attached to and her desire to see different places was stronger than her slowly developing friendships.

In those days the ride to Strobl with a horse-drawn carriage took half a day. The journey there seemed like a long trip to the young woman, who was now twenty years old. All of her belongings no longer fit into the little wooden suitcase, but Johanna Raudaschl still did not have much luggage with her as she moved into her room at the Engljähringer. She got along well with the new female boss, who was young and open-minded. Here they no longer used only the three S's 'sand, soda, and soap' for cleaning; they also had proper cleaning products and the kitchen was well equipped. With the progressing electrification,

a major upheaval was soon to take place in the household. Johanna was not afraid of anything new. She took in everything with curiosity and continued to work conscientiously on herself and her cooking skills. She even learned how to do some of the work rarely performed by women, such as slaughtering, because she thought it was important to know what parts of the cow, pig, or sheep were of the highest quality and what their texture should be, in order to bring out the best flavor.

Wherever there were lakes, such as in the Salzkammergut, fish was always popular as a special delicacy. Although Johanna had already prepared fish, in Strobl she became familiar with new variations, spices, and ingredients. This 'dowry' served her very well later for the fish connoisseurs at the Trapp house.

Johanna Raudaschl's recipe collection expanded in size and content during this time. She also wrote about everyday occurrences, some more unusual, some maybe even strange: 'During the night,' she once wrote, 'there was a knocking on the window of my little room. I was scared to death!' This was no wonder because the Engljähringer house was right next to the

The 16-year-old Johanna during her apprenticeship.

cemetery and Johanna's window looked out onto the graves, so it was actually a quiet area. 'Had the dead risen? I hardly dared to move. As the knocking became louder and I could no longer sleep, I went to the window and saw a grave cross. A wooden one. One from the grave of someone who had just recently passed away. I felt like I was paralyzed because the voices I heard did not fit in at all with the peace of the graveyard. Someone called "Hannerl!" And so I gathered all my courage, opened the window and looked out. One of the journeymen and two other workers from the butcher's shop stood below. They had been out partying so late that the door was locked and they couldn't get in. So they had unceremoniously pulled the grave cross out of the fresh mound of earth and knocked on the window with it.' Johanna quickly opened the door for them from within and darted back to her little room. Fortunately, this only happened once and they greatly appreciated that she did not report the incident to the master.

However, on November 9, 1928 Johanna Raudaschl took up a new position at her own request. From Lake Attersee to Lake Wolfgangsee, her path now took her to the shore of Lake Mondsee. This was no longer at an inn, but a private situation as a cook and housekeeper for the Hollweger sawmill in St. Lorenz. Here she ran the entire household on her own and cooked several times a day for 20 to 30 people. Grete Hollweger was glad to confirm that she fulfilled this task with special diligence. She also confirmed that the young woman distinguished herself through her 'decorous behavior.'

In her position as sole responsible housekeeper and cook for 20 to 30 people, Johanna Raudaschl has gained my fullest confidence through her particular diligence and loyalty as well as decorous behavior. I would therefore highly recommend her to anyone.

Grete Hollweger

Whenever it was possible, Johanna spent her free days at Lake Attersee. In Unterach she had a mass read on March 2, 1930 – which was a Sunday and the 10th anniversary of her grandmother's death. Johanna also returned often to Nussdorf; the reason can only be guessed at, but she may well have fallen in love with the young heir to a hereditary farm.

At this time, political events began to have a stronger influence than ever before on the life of Johanna Raudaschl. Even if the effects of the First World War had not been especially tangible in the rural solitude of the Holzberg farm, she now had to directly experience the shadows that the world economic crisis and the emerging Third Reich were casting. From 1929 onwards, many factories were closed also in Austria. The numbers of unemployed became enormous. Tourism declined. Although it had flourished during the 1920s in the Salzkammergut and the mountain regions of Upper Austria and Salzburg, the economic crisis and political uncertainties now led to a major setback. Workers knocked at the doors of the Hollweger every day to ask for work, no matter what type. These were not just trained woodcutters but also included many innkeepers. Hoteliers from the Gastein Valley who had once been wealthy took jobs as day laborers. The Hollweger took on many of them and inexperienced workers having accidents was soon part of the daily agenda. Everything ended up with the housekeeper – Johanna Raudaschl – who became like nurse and good Samaritan rolled into one, also offering everyone warm meals.

Georg Ritter von Trapp, born April 4, 1880 in what is now Croatia, died on May 30th, 1947 in Boston.

Aristocratic guests hardly came to the region any longer. Even if the aristocracy had been officially abolished in 1919, certain circles still carried the aura of exclusivity and – despite the abolition – things would probably still remain this way for a while. The fact that Baron von Trapp was in the Salzkammergut to hunt in the autumn of 1930 was the number one topic everywhere. Many people admired Georg von Trapp, who had been a respected commander of the Imperial and Royal submarine fleet in World War One and decorated with all the conceivable orders, medals, and distinctions of his day. Everyone also knew that he had recently remarried after the death of his first wife Agathe Whitehead, had sired his eighth child, a little daughter, and headed a manorial estate with many servants back home in Salzburg. That Johanna Raudaschl would be introduced to the Baron, that he would even invite her to Salzburg and spontaneously offer her the prospect of a position at his house – the now 25-year-old saw this as a wonderful act of providence and the fulfillment of all her dreams.

Sturgeon filet en papillote with herbs

1 1/3 lb (600 g)	sturgeon filet (alternatively catfish or pike), skin removed
3–4 tbsp	mixed herbs (parsley, rosemary, sage, thyme, dill) finely chopped
5	anchovy filets (in oil)
	butter
	salt, pepper

Season the sturgeon filet with salt and pepper, then rub with the finely chopped herbs. Spread butter on parchment paper and place the fish on it. Fold paper from top like a bag and close tightly with kitchen yarn.

Cook in oven at 350°F (180°C) for 15–20 minutes. Finely chop anchovy filets and brown slightly in a bit of butter. When finished cooking, open the parchment paper lengthwise from the top, drizzle anchovy butter on the fish, and leave the bag open. Continue to bake in the oven for another 5 minutes.

This dish is wonderful served with broccoli and parsley potatoes.

First day at the Trapp house

With a new hat and 'light dress'

The Trapp family experienced eventful times in those days. In 1925, three years after the tragic death of his wife Agathe Whitehead, Baron Georg von Trapp with his seven children – Rupert, Agathe, Maria, Werner, Hedwig, Johanna, and Martina – finally moved to Salzburg after taking some detours. The family lived in a beautiful big villa somewhat outside of the city in the district of Aigen. The two eldest sisters, Agathe and Maria, shared a spacious room with two desks where they did their homework in the afternoons. The older children – Rupert, Werner, Agathe, and Maria – had long outgrown the age in which they needed a nanny. A resolute housekeeper and other personnel, who lived in their own rooms on the second floor of the house, kept the house in order. Daughter Maria was in poor health at that time. After recovering from scarlet fever, she still had heart problems and much difficulty in mastering the 45-minute walk to school at the high school run by Ursuline nuns. She finally became too weak to even participate in classes, which gave her concerned father the idea of hiring a private teacher for her.

Maria Augusta Kutschera, then 21 years old, came to the house to teach Maria. For this commitment, she had left – presumably 'on loan' for ten months – the Benedictine Monastery of Nonnberg, where she was completing her time as a postulant, simultaneously working as a teacher and governess in the school there. But in the end she never returned to convent life again. Maria Augusta was always addressed with her second name of 'Fräulein Gustl' at the convent because another postulant was called 'Fräulein Maria'. So 'Fräulein Gustl' was brought to the villa at Aigen by Baron von Trapp, and first spent many hours with just Maria, who had been entrusted to her as a student. She later also taught the little Johanna

Johanna Raudaschl in 1931, when she was already working for the Trapp Family in Salzburg.

von Trapp. At the start, she only met the rest of the family during meals. Because all the children were so musically talented and had always liked to play music with their papa as often as possible, she began to gradually teach them folk songs.

The relationships deepened. On November 26, 1927, the 47-year-old Baron Georg von Trapp married Maria Augusta Kutschera, who was 25 years younger, in the church of the Nonnberg convent. In 1929 and 1931, two more daughters – Rosmarie and Eleonore (called 'Lorli') – were born. Their son Johannes Georg came into the world as the tenth child in 1939.

The wedding of the Trapps on November 26, 1927 at the Nonnberg Convent.

These were years of many changes, and a story which has become a popular myth, a story often told, changed, and – much to the regret of those involved – greatly distorted. And this is the very period when my grandmother Johanna Raudaschl entered into the service of the Trapps: 1931. Despite all the upheavals in international politics, this was still a reasonably good year for the family: a year in which they had much excitement behind them but many changes still ahead of them; a year characterized by esteem and still relative wealth, but also by gratitude and humility; a year filled with looking back at the past, and with dark premonitions of the future.

Johanna Raudaschl had already traveled to Salzburg for the first time on April 8, 1931. She had, as she meticulously entered in her little notebook under 'Expenses,' spent seven schillings on the ticket and met with Baron von Trapp in the city to agree on the details of her employment. She was to receive 80 schillings a month, which appeared to be quite appropriate, considering her free room and board, as well as the high rate of unemployment. The Baron formulated his ideas clearly and precisely and Johanna agreed – or rather, they shook hands formally, and

Captain von Trapp – once a seaman, always a seaman – warmly welcomed her 'on board'. Johanna spent the rest of the day exploring the city, which – as she knew – was often called the 'Rome of the North' because of its many churches. She had already heard a great deal about Salzburg. Now she had the chance to see it with her own eyes for the first time. With a reverent attitude, she visited one house of God after another. Deeply devout as she was, she wanted to give thanks for having found such a good position here, and during her walk through Salzburg she combined the pleasure of seeing the impressive sights with her personal need – to give heartfelt thanks to God.

About two months and some days later, on Saturday 6 June 1931, 'Hannerl' – as everyone here soon called her as well – moved into the villa in Aigen. It was the biggest and most distinguished house that she had ever seen on the inside. It was full of Persian carpets and heavy old furniture, sweeping staircases and countless doors. When she came to the house for the first time six years earlier to assume her teaching position, Maria Augusta Kutschera's reaction may have been similar to Johanna's. Neither of them had lived in a large family or in such a distinguished environment up to that time. Whether compared with the countryside or the convent, the Trapp estate made a lasting impression. In any case, at first Johanna felt very small, lost, and somewhat out of place in the high rooms. She had bought herself a new hat – for about 16 schillings – and a new, 'light dress' – for about

29 schillings – especially for the occasion of her first day at work. Why, she asked herself, had she in particular been chosen, although so many others had wanted this position? Luck? Providence? Whatever the reason, she was here now and wanted to give of her best. Other cooks had already taken care of the family. There was much talk about a certain Resi, a

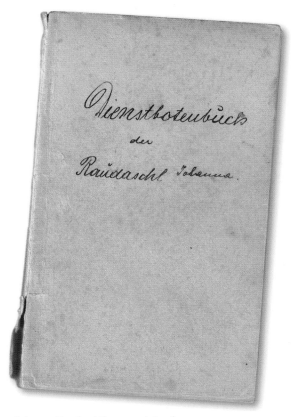

Johanna Raudaschl's servant's book.

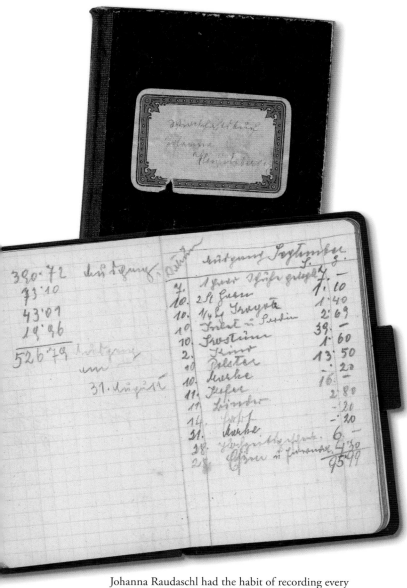

Johanna Raudaschl had the habit of recording every expenditure in a little notebook. The young cook was presumably in a shopping mood on September 10, 1931 because she spent 39 schillings on a dress.

quirky former ship's cook who had always entertained them well with her pirate stories. Other cooks might come after her, but they would be happy with HER. That was the goal that Johanna Raudaschl set for herself at the time, one to which she remained true, and which she ultimately attained.

Shortly before Johanna took up her position, Baroness von Trapp had given birth to her second daughter, Eleonore, in May 1931. She had delivered 'Lorli', like Rosmarie before her, at home under the expert instruction of her midwife Ms. Vogel. Eleonore's birth was astonishingly quick, a characteristic that would also remain with the impetuous child later in life. The young mother dedicated much time and attention – with the devoted assistance of the 14-year-old Hedwig – to the care of the newborn and her two-year-old sister. Also in spring 1931, the two oldest siblings, Rupert and Agathe, had completed their school education. Their father sent them 'out into the world', as he said, 'to expand their horizon'. They both spent some weeks with the relatives of their deceased mother in southern England, so that for a while there were only six children – Maria, Werner, Hedwig, Johanna, Martina, and Rosmarie – to be fed. They quickly began to value Hannerl's fare and to praise it to the skies. They even speculated, as my grandmother roguishly recorded, that poor Rupert and Agathe probably had some rather unfamiliar food set in front of them in distant England, while at home they frequently had apple strudel and other popular desserts in addition to the delicious meat and fish dishes on their table. The work in the kitchen was more refined and demanding than anything that had gone before.

Things were quiet, orderly, and tasteful here. Even if there was always much to do and Johanna Raudaschl's working days were long, she still loved the atmosphere of the house, especially the music and singing. In the evenings, when the family gathered around the open fireplace, Baron von Trapp played first violin, Maria and – after his return from England – Rupert accompanied him on the accordion. Like the Baroness Maria Augusta, Agathe played the guitar and the younger girls learned to play the violin. In addition to Mozart, they played Handel, Haydn, and Corelli on a regular basis. Johanna liked the children, whom she obviously could hear more often than she saw them in the rambling estate – unless they came by the kitchen for a sample.

Johanna Raudaschl got along well with the rest of the staff, which amounted to nine servants: domestic servants, chambermaids, kitchen helps, gardeners, and an English governess. The Baron encountered her with kindly reserve. There was rarely an exchange beyond a deferential nodding and greeting on the part of Johanna and a friendly response by the head of the household. But Johanna had a relationship with much esteem, that was almost a friendship, with the vivacious, charming Baroness Maria Augusta von Trapp, who was

five months younger. She was soon permitted to hold Lorli – the name Eleonore seemed much too long for such a tiny being – in her arms for the first time and recounted with much emotion: 'a delightful child with dark locks and lively dark eyes'. And slowly but surely, Johanna began to long for offspring of her own.

Maria Augusta von Trapp also appeared to value Johanna's presence so much because, as she openly admitted, she was not very good at running the household and was happy to have enough reliable personnel around her. Because her parents died when she was young, Maria Augusta had spent her childhood at boarding school, and the secluded convent life was not especially suited to teaching her the basics of housework or cooking. That obviously changed in the course of the years. As Baroness von Trapp, she grew into her tasks as mother of the family and lady of the house. She also learned some theoretical knowledge from books, but was thankful for any support that was offered her. And Johanna's almost inexhaustible wealth of recipes for 'simple and fine food' was one of the sources of inspiration that she liked to draw upon.

Instead of dealing with the household, Baroness von Trapp preferred to be outside with the children, playing volleyball with them or taking long hikes. The children – especially the hardworking, determined Maria – were often in a predicament as a result because all these activities hardly left them time for their homework. Johanna also had to organize her work well, but was in many ways also caught up in the customs of the house. For example, she also discovered hiking and on July 31 – as she proudly noted – for the first time climbed the nearby legendary Untersberg, almost two thousand meters high.

At the same time, the desire to establish a family of her own and have many children began to take vague form in Johanna, in view of the family warmth and security that, having grown up as an only child, she had never known and yet had so painfully missed. Since her years of apprenticeship at the Wiesinger in Nussdorf, she had probably had her eye on a possible marriage candidate. In any case, she returned there time and again. Her notes reveal where her heart led her on quite a regular basis during this eventful summer of 1931: 'August 9, trip to Nussdorf', 'August 18, trip to Nussdorf', 'August 28, trip to Nussdorf', 'September 14, trip to Nussdorf'. Despite all her thriftiness, the relatively high expenditures for 'stationery', 'envelopes', 'cards' and 'stamps' speak for themselves.

The Trapp Family a few months before fleeing to the USA.

Apple cake in a casserole with crumble topping

Crumble topping

Beat butter with sugar, vanilla sugar, salt, and cinnamon until soft, mix in almonds and flour, and then leave to stand in a cool place.

Apple cake

Cream butter, sugar, and vanilla sugar well, then gradually whisk in the eggs. Mix flour with baking powder and sift into the mixture.

Add milk until it becomes a foamy batter. Carefully add the diced apples with a wooden spoon. Pour the mixture into a buttered and floured form of about 10 x 8 inches and bake in a preheated oven for 15 minutes at 340°F (170°C).

Crumble the topping with your hands, sprinkle onto the cake together with almond slivers, and bake for another 25–35 minutes until done. Total baking time 40–50 minutes.

Apple cake

2 cups (350 g)	apples, peeled and cut into large cubes, soaked in lemon juice
2 3/4 cup (250 g)	pastry flour
3/5 cup (150 g)	butter
1 1/8 cups (150 g)	powdered sugar
3	eggs
1/2 cup (125 ml)	cold milk
2 tsp (8 g)	vanilla sugar
5 tsp (16 g)	baking powder

Crumble topping

1/3 cup (90 g)	butter, very soft
1/2 cup (90 g)	granulated sugar
1/2 cup (45 g)	almonds, ground
3/5 cup (65 g)	all-purpose flour
1 pinch	of salt
1 pinch	of cinnamon, ground
3 tbsp	almond slivers
1 tsp (4 g)	vanilla sugar

1 3/5 cup (150 g) pastry flour
1 1/2 cup (150 g) all-purpose flour
1 tbsp (15 g)   fresh yeast or
                2 tsp (5 g) dry yeast
1/3 cup (45 g) powdered sugar
1/2–1 cup (125–200 ml) milk and
                whipping cream in a
                50:50 mixture
1 tbsp   sour cream
                salt
                butter for the
                dumpling pan
1   egg
1/3 cup (80 g) butter, melted for
                spreading
1/2 jar   plum or apricot jam
                mixed with a bit
                of rum

Sweet buns filled with jam

To make the sweet buns (called Buchteln or Wuchteln), mix the two types of flour and sift so that it becomes very fine. Make a sponge, mixing the yeast with 1 tsp of powdered sugar, 3 tbsp of lukewarm milk, and a bit of flour. Cover with a towel and leave to rise in a warm place for about 30 minutes. Stir the rest of the ingredients into the sponge with a wooden spoon. Mix with the spoon until the dough is smooth and has bubbles. Cover the dough with a towel and let rest for another half hour.

Butter the sides of a deep baking dish and cover the bottom well with melted butter. Roll out the yeast dough on a floured work surface until it is about half a finger thick. Use a pastry cutter with a diameter of approx. 2 inches to cut out circles. Place 1/2 to 1 tsp of plum or apricot jam mixed with a bit of rum at the center of the dough circle and then close the dough around it. Dip into the melted butter with the pinched-together ends at the bottom and line them up in the baking dish. Repeat this process until the baking dish is completely full.

Cover the sweet dumplings and leave to rise for another 20 minutes, then brush with melted butter. Preheat the oven to 350°F (180°C) and bake the sweet dumplings for about 25–30 minutes in the lower half of the oven. Brush with melted butter once again at the end of the baking time.

Serve the freshly baked sweet buns with powdered sugar and vanilla sauce while they are still warm.

Beef broth with semolina strudel

Place soup vegetables with onion halves, beef bones, and marrow bones in a large pot with cold water and bring to a boil. Salt the broth and add the stewing beef. Simmer lightly without a lid until soft for about 2–3 hours.

Remove the meat and use separately. Strain the broth through a sieve and salt to taste.

Semolina Strudel
Beat butter well with egg yolks until foamy. Mix in sour cream and semolina. Cover the mixture and leave to rest for about 30 minutes. Then beat egg whites with a pinch of salt until stiff and fold into the mixture.

Sauté parsley in butter. Brush the prepared strudel dough with the butter-parsley mixture, spread the semolina mixture onto it, and roll up the dough.

Place strudel on a cookie sheet covered with parchment paper, brush with egg, and bake until golden in the preheated oven at 350°F (180°C).

Cut strudel into pieces, decorate with chives and serve in broth.

Broth

2 quarts (2 liter)	water
1	onion, halved and well-browned on cut side
1 lb (500 g)	stewing beef (from leg or shoulder, etc.)
1/2 lb (200 g)	beef bones and marrow bones root vegetables, cut into large pieces (carrot, parsley root, celeriac, leek, parsley)
1	bay leaf
10	peppercorns
3	juniper berries
1	pinch of nutmeg
	salt
	chives

Semolina Strudel

3 tbsp (40 g)	butter
2	eggs
1/2 cup (125 ml)	sour cream
1 tbsp	parsley, finely chopped
1/2 cup (100 g)	semolina
1	pinch of salt
	strudel dough
2 tbsp (25 g)	butter

1 1/2 lbs (600 g) brisket
1 tbsp   butter

Almond horseradish
1 cup (250 ml)   beef broth
1 cup (40 g)   diced rolls
2 tsp (10 ml)   whipping cream
1   egg
1   egg yolk
3 tbsp   horseradish (from
                  the jar)
1 tbsp   almonds, ground
2 tbsp   almond slivers
                  butter
                  horseradish, freshly
                  grated
                  chives, chopped

Brisket with almond-horseradish crust

Boil brisket in beef broth until soft (about 3 hours). Melt some butter in a roasting pan, slice the cooked brisket, and place in pan.

Almond horseradish: bring beef broth, diced rolls, and whipping cream to a boil, and then blend well with a handheld blender. Boil once more and then whisk in horseradish, ground almonds, egg, egg yolk, and almond slivers. Spread a thick coat of the almond horseradish over the top of the brisket slices. Drizzle some melted butter over it. Broil in oven at 430°F (220°C) until golden brown.

Crisp root vegetables, creamed cabbage, and potatoes go well with this. Serve the brisket sprinkled with some freshly grated horseradish and chopped chives.

Salzburger Nockerl
[soufflé dessert]

This original way of preparing the Salzburger Nockerl in the pan has almost been forgotten.

Separate egg yolks and whites, melt butter, and slightly heat milk with vanilla sugar. Beat egg whites with the sugar in a large bowl until stiff. Carefully fold egg yolks with half of the melted butter, half of the vanilla milk, and the flour into the beaten egg whites. Heat the rest of the butter in a cast-iron pan, pour in the mixture, and cover with a lid. When the mixture is slightly browned on the bottom, cut out large mounds with a pancake spatula, turn and bake covered until the other side also becomes slightly brown.

Pour the rest of the vanilla milk over it and let stand briefly so that the milk can be absorbed and the soufflé can rise a bit more.

Sprinkle with powdered sugar and serve immediately.

3	eggs
1 tbsp	flour
1 tbsp	granulated sugar
1/4 cup (60 g)	butter
1/3 cup (100 ml)	milk
1 tsp	vanilla sugar

For the masters and for the staff

... and yet, all men are equal

Salzburg had about 40,000 residents in 1931. During the winter the city seemed quiet and sleepy, but even back then, it blossomed every year into the 'Metropolis of Music' in the summer. Johanna Raudaschl had never before come into contact with the kind of cultural life that she experienced in the Trapp house. In July and August, the city was full of artists and music fans from all over the world, who had come to attend the Festival founded in 1920. About 60,000 visitors from other places were counted in 1931, and revenues from their expenditures – 'on average 100 schillings per person' – totaling six million, were calculated for Salzburg and Austria. Many things actually just covered up the true problems of the times, yet being a part of this – even if just on the sidelines – greatly influenced my grandmother's life from that time on.

The 175th birthday of Wolfgang Amadeus Mozart was celebrated in 1931, with five of his operas on the program, including three new productions. Alexander Moissi played – for the last time, as was soon revealed – Jedermann (Everyman) on the Domplatz (Cathedral Square). Stars like Arturo Toscanini, Richard Strauss, Bruno Walter, and Lotte Lehmann were there. Lotte Lehmann, with her connections and her legendary remark that the Trapp children sang from 'golden throats', was later to point the way for the career of the singing Trapp family.

Many leading figures of the Festival, both artists and audience, came to visit at the genteel villa in Aigen. Close and more distant relatives were invited, or simply invited themselves. The von Trapp couple played an active role in the social occasions and was often their focus as the hosts. Baroness Maria Augusta attracted people with her remarkable personality. She had a special personal magnetism, which we would probably call 'charisma' today, and she visibly enjoyed the attention that she received everywhere, while the Baron preferred to stay in the background.

The Baroness often did not make it easy for those around her because of her firm convictions. She rejected any type of alcohol consumption, as well as smoking. This strict rejection was not based on general health reasons, because these had not yet been publicized at that time. They were just her personal reservations, and she emphatically insisted upon them. In addition, after a protracted illness that had 'affected her kidneys', Maria Augusta von Trapp was forced to abide by a strict diet for years: no meat, no eggs, and very little salt or spices. Johanna Raudaschl was naturally aware of this and followed the 'stipulations' that she had been given. Although not exactly an epicure and unable to eat certain things, the Baroness still reserved the right to personally decide the daily meal plan and select the food 'for the masters and for the staff' together with her cook.

This often occurred quite late in the morning, although the main meal was eaten at noon rather than in the evening. So it was practically at the last minute when Johanna heard whether guests would join the family for a meal and what should be served. It could easily happen that visitors had arrived unexpectedly and the schnitzels that the Baroness had ordered from the butcher the day before

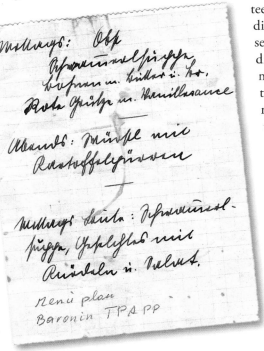

One of Johanna Raudaschl's notes with the lunch menu for the masters and for the staff.

were not sufficient. Then, even in a city like Salzburg, it was not so simple to quickly find something fitting and tasty.

Nevertheless, Johanna Raudaschl – as she often liked to tell – mounted her rickety bicycle and rode along the Salzach into the city. She always managed somehow to put a meal on the table that was not only on time but also of the best quality. The old-established fish shop on the Hanuschplatz and the stalls at the farmers' market were always guarantees for the best merchandise. Depending on the season, vegetable farmers displayed their assortments while other people, trying to earn a little bit of money during these hard times, offered cheaply mushrooms they had gathered or fresh blueberries (which turned everything blue).

On some of these days, Johanna Raudaschl already started work at 5 a.m. and didn't finish until the evening. Despite good organization and many helpful servants, cooking for social gatherings was a considerable challenge – extremely time-consuming and also physically strenuous. Johanna sometimes had to stir ten saucepans at the same time.

Although they already had electric lighting and even a modern gas cooker to warm something up quickly between meals, the majority of the food was prepared on the large stove that stood at the center of the kitchen. The stove was still fueled with wood, which meant that it did not have any temperature regulation. This obviously caused problems. Quite a bit of experience was required to make sure everything finished cooking at just the right time and nothing burned.

A holy card out of Johanna Raudaschl's recipe books.

A later look at Johanna Raudaschl's cookbooks from back then revealed that the well-worn volumes contained not only recipes but a variety of holy cards to provide spiritual guidance, hastily written notes, and yellowed newspaper clippings. One of the clippings serves as an example, since it says much about the spirit of those times, as well as highlighting the character of the cook who was always interested in further educating herself and doing the best for those who were entrusted to her: 'Cooking with Electricity', was the title of an article published on November 14, 1931 in the Salzburger Chronik newspaper: 'The contest between electricity and gas is also quietly intensifying for dominance in the kitchen since gas has already been more or less replaced by the much more convenient electric light as a means of illumination in Salzburg. On Friday, November 13, 1931, a demonstration of cooking with electricity took place at the congress center. It was presented by Ms. Wimmer, who had already rendered great services as Salzburg's first cook to use electricity. The entire preparation of a meal cooked with electricity was demonstrated: 3.3 pounds of roast pork, rice, stewed fruit, and – as a dessert – a Swiss roll were cooked to perfection in less than two hours and served to those present as a very well-received sample.' Was Johanna Raudaschl one of those present? Probably not. But how open she was to the developments and changes of her time, as well as her participation in them, is definitely shown by these carefully archived lines.

It would also be a long time before there was this kind of an electric stove in the Trapp house and cooking remained a very arduous task as a result. This did not change the fact that before each meal for 'the masters' was served, the staff had to be fed separately. Their meal was usually a different, simpler one. It consisted of soup and no more than one additional course, while the family and guests had a dessert, which was eaten in the parlor after the meal. This is where the table talk took place, as Johanna Raudaschl later remembered, whereas meals around the heavy oak table were usually eaten in silence.

Johanna had had little experience in distinguished houses up to that time, so there actually was no basis for comparison. However, she always mentioned how open and honest the appreciation was that she received for her work at the stove and how happy it made her. This praise meant a great deal to her and she felt that a special trait of the Baroness lay behind it: herself from a simple background, Maria Augusta's considerable reservations about the aristocracy and those who thought they were better than others continued for quite a while. All human beings were equal for Maria Augusta. Whether family or staff, she placed value on treating everyone equally – with the same strictness and the same consistency. In the early years, her attitude had given rise to all kinds of tensions, since her in-laws included aristocratic families that owned manorial estates, and even castles. It took some time for her to discover, to her own astonishment, that even 'these aristocrats', as she called them, were basically very normal, amiable, and warm-hearted people and not as aloof as she had feared. This was a life experience that ultimately led Maria Augusta to also accept the title of Baroness for herself.

Even if Johanna Raudaschl thought she could occasionally glimpse the former enthusiastic free-thinking spirit behind the stern façade of her employer, she was required to address her as 'Baroness'. That spirit had already moved the Reverend Abbess of the Nonnberg convent to recommend to the postulant 'Fräulein Gustl' that she take a secular path in life despite all the young woman's admittedly sincere piety. In any case, there was still a remainder of nonconformist behavior that manifested itself when the Baroness von Trapp preferred to use her fingers instead of silver tongs for putting sugar lumps in her coffee …

Veal Ragout with Mushrooms

Sauté onion in butter until golden brown. Cut veal into cubes, add to pan and briefly cook until the meat is evenly browned. Mix in tomato paste, mustard, lemon zest, and salt. Immediately pour in the white wine and broth, then cover and steam over low heat for about 20–30 minutes until soft. Add chopped mushrooms and simmer for a few minutes. Mix whipping cream with one tsp of flour and use it to thicken the ragout. Finish with a pinch of mace, pepper, and finely chopped parsley.

Serve the veal ragout with brussel sprouts, rice with peas, bread dumplings, or potatoes.

1 1/3 lb (600 g)	veal
1	medium-sized onion, finely chopped
2 tbsp	butter
1 tbsp	tomato paste
1 tbsp	mustard
1/2 lb (200 g)	mushrooms (porcini, chanterelle, or other mushrooms), coarsely chopped
1/2 cup (125 ml)	white wine
1 cup (250 ml)	beef or veal broth
1 tsp	flour
1/2 cup (125 ml)	whipping cream
	parsley
	salt, pepper, mace
	zest of 1/4 lemon

Cod in sauce

Lightly brown onion in butter in a roasting pan. Add parsley and marjoram and immediately pour in fish stock. Then add salt, lemon zest, and mace. Season fish with salt and pepper and put it in the roasting pan. Cover and simmer in the oven at 280°F (140°C) for about 20–30 minutes. Occasionally baste fish with sauce.

Cut the cod into thick slices and serve with parsley potatoes, spinach, zucchini, or braised tomatoes.

1 1/3 lb (600 g)	cod (in one piece with carcass)
2 tbsp	butter
	zest of half a lemon
1	onion, finely chopped
1 tsp	marjoram, freshly chopped
2 tbsp	parsley, chopped
1/2 tsp	mace
1 cup (250 ml)	fish stock
	salt, pepper

3 1/4 cups (500 g) blueberries
3   eggs, seperated
1/2 cup (70 g) powdered sugar
1   pinch of salt
1 1/3 cup (140 g) flour
Approx. 1 cup (250 ml) milk
                butter for frying

Blueberry dumplings

Beat sugar and egg yolks with mixer until foamy. Add flour, and enough milk to make a creamy thick batter. Then mix in the blueberries. Beat the egg whites until stiff with a pinch of salt. Finally, fold in the stiffly whipped egg whites.

Heat pan with plenty of butter and use a spoon to put in the individual dumplings, which should have a diameter of about 2–3 inches. Cook until slightly brown on both sides. Sprinkle with powdered sugar and serve immediately.

Torte

1/2 cup (130 g)	butter
3/4 cup (100 g)	powdered sugar
1/2 cup (85 g)	cornstarch
5	eggs
1/2 cup (120 g)	chocolate (semi-sweet with 70% cocoa content)
1 tsp	baking powder
1 pinch	salt
1 tbsp	granulated sugar

Chocolate icing

4–6 tbsp	milk
1/2 cup (75 g)	powdered sugar
1/3 cup (100 g)	semi-sweet or baking chocolate
1 1/2 tbsp (20 g)	butter

Chocolate torte

Cream butter and sugar until foamy. Gradually add the egg yolks. Mix cornstarch with baking powder and salt and stir into the mixture. Melt chocolate in the oven and let cool before stirring into the mixture. Finally, beat the egg whites until stiff with a pinch of salt and 1 tbsp of granulated sugar. Carefully fold into the mixture.

Fill into a buttered and floured pan (8–9 inch diameter) and bake at 340°F (170°C) on the middle rack for about 40 minutes. Remove from the pan after cooling, spread with fine apricot jam, and cover with chocolate icing. This mixture can also be baked in a ribbed log-cake tin, but then it must be reduced by one-third.

For the chocolate icing, slowly heat milk, powdered sugar, and chocolate in a small pot on the stove and stir well. Finally mix in butter and cover torte with icing.

Convent crescents

Work butter into flour with the fingertips. Dissolve yeast in milk (makes a creamy paste). Then blend yolks, sugar, salt, and yeast well into the flour-butter mixture. Let dough rest in a cool place for about 1 hour.

Roll out dough to about 1/4 inch thick. Cut out triangles with a side length of 3–4 inches and fill with 1/2 tsp of blackberry jam. Roll up dough and form crescent. Place on cookie sheet with parchment paper. Crescents will rise when baking, so space them out evenly on the sheet. Bake until golden in a 320°F (160°C) preheated oven on the middle rack for about 15–20 minutes. Leave to cool.

Beat 3 egg whites with a dash of lemon juice until foamy but not too stiff. Fill the mixture into the piping bag with the medium-sized tip and top the cooled convent crescents with a one-inch layer. Sprinkle with coarse granulated sugar and brown until golden in a preheated oven set to top heat at 430°F (220°C).

2 1/3 cup (210 g)	pastry flour
1 cup (210 g)	butter
3	egg yolks
1 tbsp	sugar
1 pinch	salt
1 1/3 tbsp (20 g)	fresh yeast or 1 tbsp (7 g) yeast, active dry
1–2 tsp	milk
3	egg whites
1 dash	lemon juice
	blackberry jam
	coarse granulated sugar for sprinkling
	flour for rolling out the dough

Tea sticks

Work all of the ingredients into a dough on a board. Roll out dough and form sticks that are about the length and diameter of a pencil. Brush water onto them and sprinkle with granulated sugar or cinnamon. Bake until golden at 340°F (170°C) for about 8–10 minutes.

1/2 cup (100 g)	butter
3/4 cup (100 g)	powdered sugar
1 1/2 cup (200 g)	flour
1	egg white
	some lemon or orange zest
	granulated sugar
	cinnamon

Pine-nut (Pignoli) crescents

Beat egg whites over steam with a pinch of salt. Very slowly add the granulated sugar to the beaten egg whites and continue beating until the mixture is warm and creamy. Then continue beating without heat for about 5 more minutes.

Stir in the almonds and fill mixture into piping bag with round, medium-sized tip. Cover cookie sheet with parchment paper and pipe the crescents onto it. Sprinkle thickly with pignoli. Bake in the oven at 230°F (110°C) for about 60–70 minutes.

It is easier to get the crescents of the parchment paper if you allow the cookie sheet to cool down for a few minutes.

3	egg whites
3/4 cup (150 g)	granulated sugar
1	pinch of salt
1 cup (100 g)	almonds, ground
1 1/2 cup (200 g)	pignoli (peeled pine nuts)

In harmony with the Trapp Family

Celebrating occasions as they arise

Johanna Raudaschl was distinguished by her quiet, modest manner and friendly nature. Throughout the year, her cooking was perfectly geared to the succession of religious festivals and the customs of the Catholic Church, as they were introduced into the Trapp household by Baroness Maria Augusta and soon accepted by the family. She had brought many changes and new everyday habits with her. Baron von Trapp had supposedly only converted to Catholicism through his marriage to her. Of course, Johanna Raudaschl didn't have to adapt at all. Since she herself had strict religious convictions, these qualities of diligence, thriftiness, and willingness to sacrifice were already second nature to her. The traditions that were upheld and cultivated here had always been the same as her own, together with a heartfelt piety that determined how she lived her life. This harmony with Baroness von Trapp was one of the foundations for the special relationship between the two women, so different and yet in some ways kindred spirits.

In addition to the ecclesiastical year, the immutable natural cycle of growth and decay also determined the menu in a certain sense, even in the city. One portion of the extensive parks around the Trapp villa was used for agriculture. They cultivated vegetables and fruit, and happy chickens were kept in sheds which the Trapp sons had built on their own. Only ingredients that grew in the fields and were in season were used in the kitchen. So that the food would keep as long as possible, there was a pantry – large and spacious like a small grocery store, with countless drawers and shelves – in addition to the 'cold cellar'. A mysterious fragrance hovered above it all – a mixture of dried herbs and mushrooms, garlic and onions that had been braided into plaits and hung from the ceiling. Preserved jam, stewed fruit, pickles, and beetroots had been stored in jars and were ready to be used.

Dried apple slices, plums, and walnuts were stored there. The egg rack was always filled to bursting so that there was no need to economize. Beating ten to twelve eggs into a batter was quite usual in the kitchen of that time, despite all the frugality. Thanks to the flock of chickens in the garden, they were self-sufficient in this respect. The budget for the household did not need to cover either eggs or chicken, so it was often on

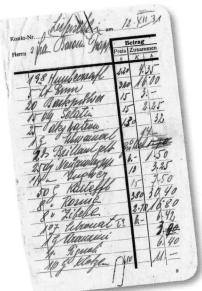

A delivery slip from the Trapp household.

the menu in all of its possible variations. Johanna Raudaschl concocted her own delicious chicken dishes. When the meal was prepared, a bell rang in the Trapp house and everyone came to the table. The Baron actually did use a whistle with a sequence of notes for each child, as Johanna Raudaschl confirmed. However, it was not a military command but rather an endearing call that the father had devised for his children on the rambling estate; but the bell was always used for meals. During the time when all bells were silent – from Maundy Thursday to Easter Sunday – it was a wooden 'rattle' that replaced the bell. Johanna found out that the family always had a fresh 'green' soup of spring herbs on Maundy Thursday. She devised an additional method of preparation to this, which was then also well received outside the Lenten fast.

Outings were on the agenda for the family. Just like Johanna, the Baron, the Baroness, and the children enjoyed cycling. They already pedaled to school every day and the previous summer they had all traveled on their bicycles to Pola, now called Pula and part of Croatia.

It took five days to reach the seaport in Istria, where Baron Georg von Trapp had previously been stationed for many years as the captain of the Imperial and Royal submarine fleet. The luggage – as the amazed Johanna discovered – had been sent by train to the vacation destination. An uncle had taken care of it. Although it was not possible to have this type of adventure during the summer of 1931, they went on many bicycle outings in the immediate and more distant surroundings. Provisions for the journey had to be prepared in the kitchen in advance so that the family could be fed en route. They loved the freshly baked bread, but everyone still was happy to have a substantial meal when they returned home. Since Johanna never knew exactly when the exhausted horde would be returning, as a precaution there was always a pot of food on the stove, patiently simmering on a small flame.

Autumn brought the hunting season. Even during her youth, Johanna had particularly enjoyed preparing game. Aristocratic hunting parties had always provided a welcome opportunity for the farmers to earn a bit on the side; this consisted of both much-needed cash for their services and payment in kind. They had to rouse the game for the guns by beating with sticks and yelling loudly. Experienced helpers who were familiar with the surroundings were also hired to retrieve the game that had been shot in rough terrain. They were rewarded with money and sometimes also a piece of the venison for the cooking pot at home. In the autumn of 1931, the only reason that Baron von Trapp parted from his children – whom he loved more than anything in the world – was to join one of these hunting parties. In addition to life on the high seas, hunting was his passion. It had been during one of these hunts, that the paths of the Baron and Johanna Raudaschl first crossed. The respected sawmill-owner Hollweger from St. Lorenz on Lake Mondsee had gone deerstalking the previous autumn, with a high-ranking hunting party that included Baron von Trapp. Hollweger had invited everyone to the 'Schüsseltrieb', a get-together after a successful hunt, at which a kind of venison stew typical of the Salzkammergut region was served. No-one prepared it so deliciously as his cook Johanna. As thanks for his hospitality, he was to lose Hannerl to the Baron, who would have liked to immediately take her with him to Salzburg. In the end, Baron von Trapp had to allow Hollweger enough time to find a suitable successor for his sizeable household, so Johanna was forced to wait six months before she could move to Salzburg.

As the months passed, there was one religious festival after another. Hardly a day passed without some significance in the calendar of the Catholic Church: the feast days of the Lord and the Blessed Virgin, and commemorations of saints and apostles. Maria Augusta von Trapp had selected the Sacred Heart festival, on the eighth day after Corpus Christi, as the 'family festival'. After celebrating mass together, they talked about the past and the future during an abundant breakfast. Later, when the family performed throughout the world as a choir, this was the day when every member had the opportunity of agreeing to stay for the coming year or to say farewell – which of course few of them did, so that the family ensemble continued for about 20 years. Since they were still just making music at home in 1931, singing was not the basis of their income but a source of joy. Plans for the future were made at the Sacred Heart festival – for Rupert's medical studies and Agathe's artistic ambitions. Already aware that everything would ultimately happen in a different way, Johanna Raudaschl later had melancholy memories of this hope for a new beginning at this June 12 meeting, just a few days after she began working there.

The birthdays were naturally special celebrations that occurred more frequently for the Trapps than in other households because of the large number of children. There was hardly a month without a birthday party. The day brought a change from the usual routine by the prospect of a special favorite meal, as well as festive clothes, rituals, and old traditions. Baroness von Trapp placed great value on making each child's birthday a special occasion. They began celebrating the evening before. Everyone in the house – family, staff, and any guests present – gathered in a semi-circle around a round table set in white, upon which were presents and a birthday cake with the corresponding number of burning candles. The birthday boy or girl then received a seasonal flower from each person in the group, making a sizeable bouquet. Then he or she had to think of a wish and blow out all the candles with one breath.

Wine pastry
3 1/3 cup (300 g) pasty flour
1 cup (250 g) butter
1/4 cup (60 ml) white wine
1/2 tsp salt
butter for brushing

Apricot-curd cheese filling
1 1/2 lbs (700 g) apricots, cut into eights (small apricots into quarters)
1/2 cup (100 g) butter
1 1/3 cup (300 g) curd cheese
3/4 cup (100 g) powdered sugar
2 eggs, separated
Cinnamon

Tip: The curd cheese should be dry, so allow to drain for some time beforehand.

Apricot-curd cheese strudel

Knead all of the ingredients into a pastry and leave to stand overnight.

For the filling, beat butter and sugar well, then blend in the curd cheese, egg yolks, and cinnamon. Fold in apricots with a wooden spoon. Finally, carefully fold in the beaten egg whites.

Then roll out the pastry on a floured counter leaving a third of it a little thicker than the rest. Spread the apricot/curd-cheese filling on the middle third and fold the thinner third and the sides over the filling; then brush the thicker third with butter and fold over so that it is on top.

Brush the strudel well with butter and bake on the middle rack in the preheated oven at 390°F (200°C) for 12 minutes. Then reduce heat to 350°F (175°C) and bake for another 20–30 minutes.

Bohemian dumplings

Dice the rolls and lightly brown in butter. Warm 1–2 tbsp of milk to lukewarm and add yeast, granulated sugar, and a bit of flour to mix into the sponge (the day before) and let it rise to double its volume.

Quickly work cold milk, egg, flour, parsley, salt, and nutmeg into a dough, add the sponge, and mix with the browned diced cubes. Let the mixture rise in a warm place for 15 minutes. Spread butter onto one side of each of the two kitchen towels. Form the mixture into two logs and roll up loosely in the towels so that they can still rise a little. Tie on both sides with kitchen yarn. Let them rest for 15 minutes.

Simmer in a large pot with plenty of salted water for about 45 minutes. Take the dumplings out of the water and remove the kitchen towels. Cut the dumplings into thick slices and lightly brown both sides in butter.

Red wine pears

Peel the ripe pears, cut them in half and remove the core with a small spoon or melon baler. In a pot, reduce red wine, port, cloves, cinnamon, ginger and sugar down to half the quantity. Sieve the liquid, add a generous dash of cassis liqueur and pour over the pears while still hot (the pear halves should be covered). Cover them and let them infuse for at least two days, occasionally turning the pears over. Before serving, reheat slightly and fill the pears with lingonberry jam.

4	day-old rolls
1	egg
3 1/2 tbsp (50 g)	butter
1/4 tsp	granulated sugar
2 tsp (10 g)	fresh yeast or
	1/2 tbsp (4 g) yeast, active dry
1–2 tbsp	lukewarm milk
1 cup (200–250 ml)	cold milk
4/5 cup (75 g)	pastry flour
1 pinch	of nutmeg
	salt
	chopped parsley
	butter to spread on
	2 kitchen towels and
	brown the cooked
	dumplings

2	pears
1 cup (250 ml)	red wine
1/2 cup (125 ml)	red port wine
1 dash	cassis liqueur (made of black currants)
4	cloves
1	cinnamon stick
1 tbsp	sugar
1–2	slices of ginger
	lingonberry jam

1 lb (500 g)	green tomatoes
2/3 lb (300 g)	white onions
3 1/2 tbsp (50 g)	salt
1 tbsp	mustard seeds
1 tbsp	whole black pepper-corns
1	bay leaf
3 tsp	sugar
1 cup (250 ml)	white vinegar
2 2/3 cup (625 ml)	water

Green tomato kraut

Green Tomato Kraut tastes great combined with a cold snack.

Finely slice the tomatoes and onions. Dissolve salt in water. Pour water over tomatoes and onions and leave to stand over night. Drain off the next day.

Bring vinegar, water with mustard, peppercorns, bay leaf, and sugar to a boil. Fill tomatoes and onions in jars and pour vinegar mixture over them until the vegetables are completely covered.

Close jars. While they are still warm, place in a large pot, cover with water, and boil for 10 minutes. This way, the green tomato kraut is sterilized and will stay fresh for a long time.

Tip: If white balsamic vinegar is used, the green tomato kraut will taste even milder. Green Tomato Kraut tastes great combined with a savory snack.

2	young chickens or chicken parts (about 2 1/2 to 3 1/3 lbs or 1.2 to 1.5 kg)
3 tbsp	oil
1 cup (200g)	onions, finely chopped
1/2 cup (100g)	smoked bacon, finely chopped
2 1/2 tbsp (20g)	hot paprika powder
	zest of 1 lemon
1 tbsp	tomato paste
2 cups (500 ml)	broth
1/2 cup (125 ml)	sour cream
1/2 cup (125 ml)	whipping cream
2 tbsp	flour
	some lemon juice
	salt

Paprika chicken

Cut chicken into pieces and brown in oil in a large roasting pan. Take out pieces of chicken and then brown onions and smoked bacon in the same roasting pan. Add the paprika, lemon zest, and tomato paste. Mix briefly and immediately pour in the broth. Add the chicken pieces and braise until soft with a closed lid for about 30 minutes.

Remove chicken meat and take off the skin. Take lemon zest out of the sauce. Mix sour cream with 2 tbsp of flour, thicken the sauce with it, and purée with the hand mixer. Stir in the whipping cream, strain the sauce, and then season to taste with salt and lemon juice. Put the chicken pieces back in the sauce and heat them once again. Serve with butter spaetzle.

Stew with beans

Soak beans in cold water over night.

Lightly brown the onion in oil, then add the meat and brown on all sides. Add the garlic, salt, pepper, caraway, and paprika. Immediately deglaze with the wine and beef broth.

After about 20 minutes, stir in the soaked beans and carrots. Let it simmer for about 30–40 minutes until the carrots are soft but firm to the bite. Dissolve cornstarch in a bit of cold water and use it to thicken the stew. Stir in the crème fraiche and parsley.

Best served with potatoes, polenta, or rice.

1 1/3 lb (600 g)	pork (from the shank or lean pork belly), diced
3 tbsp	oil
1 1/4 cup (200 g)	dried red beans, soaked
1	large onion, finely chopped
1 tbsp	paprika powder
1	clove of garlic, chopped
1 tsp	caraway, ground
1/2 cup (125 ml)	white wine
1/2 cup (125 ml)	beef broth
1 tsp	cornstarch
1/2 lb (200 g)	carrots, finely diced
1/3 cup (60 g)	crème fraiche
	salt
	pepper
	parsley, chopped

Spring herb soup

Sauté onion in butter until transparent, add flour and sauté briefly. Deglaze with vegetable broth and milk, then stir. Let it simmer for about 15–20 minutes and then purée with a handheld blender. Add liquid whipping cream and herbs. Then season, reheat, and purée once again.

Before serving the soup, top off with whipped cream. Good additions to the soup are a 'poached egg' or toasted croutons.

Eggs are 'poached' by breaking them into lightly simmering water with a dash of vinegar.

1 1/2 tbsp (20 g)	butter
2 tbsp (20 g)	pastry flour
2 1/2 cups (600 ml)	vegetable broth
1 cup (200 ml)	whipping cream
2/3 cup (150 ml)	milk
2 tbsp	onion, finely chopped
6 tbsp	herbs, finely chopped (e.g.: basil, parsley, chives, dill, lemon balm, lovage, thyme, dandelion)
4 tbsp	whipped cream salt, pepper

Saddle of venison

2 lb (800 g)	saddle of venison – remove meat from bones (reserve bones and meat scraps for sauce)
	oil for browning
	salt, pepper

Sauce

1 lb (400 g)	venison bones and meat scraps
1/3 lb (150 g)	onions, finely chopped
1/4 lb (100 g)	carrots, diced
1/4 lb (100 g)	celeriac, diced
	oil for browning
1 tbsp	tomato paste
1 tbsp	porcini powder
8	juniper berries
1 tsp	allspice
1 tbsp	peppercorns
1 tsp	caraway seeds, whole
3 tsp	cornstarch
1 cup (250 ml)	beef broth or game stock
1/2 cup (125 ml)	red wine
1/2 cup (125 ml)	red port wine
2 tbsp	lingonberries
1 tbsp	butter
	salt, pepper, sugar

Saddle of venison

Prepare the sauce first. Fry venison bones, meat scraps, carrots, and celeriac in oil in a large pot.

Add onions and fry until golden. Mix in tomato paste, spices (juniper berries, allspice, peppercorn, caraway), and lingonberries. Immediately pour in the beef broth or game stock with the red wine. Cover and let it simmer for about 90 minutes. Strain sauce through a sieve. Add port wine and porcini powder, then let it simmer for another 30 minutes without a lid. Thicken sauce with cornstarch (dissolve in a little cold water) and season to taste with pepper, salt, and a bit of sugar.

Finally, add 1 tbsp of cold butter. Season the saddle of venison with salt and pepper and brown well on all sides with some oil in a large sauce pan. Remove the meat and leave to rest for about 15 minutes. Put the sauce in the pan and bring to a boil. Place the meat in the sauce and simmer for about 5 minutes.

Remove the meat and carefully cut into thick slices. Serve with sauce.

Good side dishes for the saddle of venison are Bohemian dumplings, red cabbage, brussel sprouts, broccoli, or beans with bacon, as well as pears poached in red wine.

Poacher's ragout

Dice onion, carrots, and celeriac. Season the venison with salt and pepper and brown in hot oil. Remove meat and brown the bacon (whole), carrots, celeriac, and onion in the same pan. Add and briefly brown garlic and then stir in tomato paste. Mix in the venison with the spices and capers.

Pour in broth and add lingonberries. Then cover and simmer at low heat for about 90 minutes until soft. After about 75 minutes, remove smoked bacon and add vinegar, wine, and sugar. Simmer for another 15 minutes. Take venison out of the sauce, strain the sauce, and put the meat back in. Mix 1 tbsp of flour with the crème fraiche and thicken the sauce with it.

Serve venison ragout with Bohemian dumplings or potatoes.

1 1/3 lb (600 g)	leg of venison leg, cut into approx. 1-inch cubes
3/4 oz (20 g)	piece of smoked bacon, whole
1/2	onion, medium size
1/2 lb (200 g)	carrots
1/2 lb (200 g)	celeriac
1	bay leaf
	thyme, marjoram
4	juniper berries
1 tsp	lemon zest, finely chopped
5	vinegar capers
1	garlic clove, chopped
3 tbsp	lingonberries
	oil for browning
1 cup (250 ml)	beef broth
1 tbsp	vinegar
1/2 cup (125 ml)	red wine
1 tsp	sugar
1 tsp	tomato paste
	salt, pepper
1/3 cup (70 g)	crème fraiche
1 tbsp	flour for thickening

3 1/3 cup (280 g) almonds, ground
1 1/4 cup (280 g) butter, soft
2 egg yolks
1 egg
1 1/2 cup (200 g) powdered sugar
lemon zest
1/2 tsp cloves, ground
1/2 tsp cinnamon, ground
3 cup (280 g) flour
some milk
1 1/4 cup (250 g) red currant jam
wafers (little round circles, rice paper rounds can also be used)

Linzer Torte

Beat butter, eggs and egg yolks until creamy. Stir in almonds, powdered sugar, lemon zest, and spices. Then stir in the flour. Should the dough be to firm, add some milk.

Press 2/3 of the dough into a buttered and floured tart pan and cover with wafers. Spread jam evenly on top and use the remaining third of the dough to make a lattice-work pattern on top of the jam. Bake for about 50–60 minutes at 325°F (160°C).

My grandmother always covered the Linzer Torte with so-called 'icing' to prevent it from drying out. The subtly tart flavor harmonizes perfectly with the other ingredients.

The 'icing' is made from 3/4 cup (100 g) powdered sugar, zest of 1/2 orange (or lemon) and one egg white. Blend until it turns into a thick and creamy paste. Then add a little bit of orange (or lemon) juice and spread thinly over the tart.

Another possibility is to sprinkle slivered almonds over the 'icing' on the outer edge of the tart. Leave to dry in oven at a low temperature.

A special time

Advent and Christmas 1931 in the Trapp household

Of all the celebrations held throughout the year in the Trapp house, Christmas with its mystery was probably the one that stood out the most. This celebration not only left the strongest impression upon my grandmother Johanna Raudaschl but also, in its festive arrangement, differed the most from what she had known up to then. One reason for this was the supposedly 'rural custom' of a Christmas tree that had actually never been a part of Johanna's childhood and youth. Christmas trees had already come into fashion in Vienna during the Biedermeier period. However, they had only slowly caught on in the Austrian provinces, especially in the poorer rural regions. The situation was completely different in the Trapp villa. They decorated a tall fir tree with candies and cookies, little red apples, homemade Christmas tree ornaments, and wax candles, so it looked like it came from fairyland. Although Johanna accepted this tradition for herself and later cultivated it within her own family circle, she usually just decorated a simple branch in-

stead of a huge tree. She thought it would have been a pity to waste the tree like that.

Advent 1931: Many things were still made by hand and not bought in stores back then. There was no feverish hustle disturbing the peace required to prepare the celebration in an appropriate way. It took weeks to get body and soul in the right mood for Christmas and they made sure to take this time. In the evenings – in the glow of the candles on the Advent wreath – the family spent even more time than usual singing together – Advent hymns, because Christmas carols were reserved for Christmas Eve. The aroma of freshly baked cookies filled the air.

Advent, Johanna Raudaschl later wrote in her memoirs, became a special experience: an empty manger with straw next to it stood on a little table. If we believed we had done something good or refrained from something, she wrote, we were permitted to place a straw in the manger. By Christmas Eve, the manger was then filled to the top with straw. However, this custom wasn't just reserved for the children or the family; everyone in the house was included and encouraged to participate. This created a general mood of joyful anticipation and mutual attentiveness in the weeks leading up to the celebration.

Johanna was probably quite familiar with the custom that unmarried women picked cherry sprigs in the orchard on St. Barbara's Day, December 4, and carefully kept them watered in the hopes that they would blossom for Christmas. If they actually flowered, a wedding was predicted ... Fortunately, she managed to bring the sprigs into the warm house at the last moment because winter suddenly arrived on the night of December 4, 1931. With it came Saint Nicholas, one of the most popular saints, and patron saint of sailors. The idea that he was often accompanied by the ugly, chain-rattling 'Krampusses' was already controversial at that time, and Johanna Raudaschl later remembered that there once were vehement discussions about their significance, probably triggered by an article in the *Salzburger Chronik*, in which educators warned: 'People cannot seem to do anything in moderation. Beautiful, meaningful Saint Nicholas customs are ancient. Christian and old pagan rites have been merged into a unique synthesis that has already survived the many storms of time up to this day. However, the beauty, the deep meaning, the good purpose of an old custom is increasingly lost the further it departs from its festive idea. Saint Nicholas celebrations are rapidly becoming Krampus fests. Especially in this time of need, the kindly old figure of Saint Nicholas must be given its due respect – in as far as our age permits.'

Even in 1931, it was still possible to some extent in the Trapp household to let Saint Nicholas 'be given his due respect'. The important visitor arrived punctually and proclaimed an astonishing knowledge about everyone's good deeds from his big book, after which he distributed little bags of sweets. He assumed that words of warning to those who had not been well-behaved were adequate. The controversial rod and the scary companions did not even have to make an appearance. There were even small gifts for the servants on this occasion. The modest Johanna Raudaschl found it both touching and unforgettable that there was a table set up with gifts not just for the family but also for all the staff on Christmas Eve. In view of the very hard times, this was probably more than a Christmas miracle!

Makes 4 stollen

2.2 lb (1000 g)	pastry flour
7 tbsp (100 g)	fresh yeast or 5 tbsp (35 g) yeast, active dry
2 cups (400 ml)	lukewarm milk
1/2 tsp	granulated sugar
1 1/3 cup (300 g)	butter
1 1/2 cups (200 g)	powdered sugar
2 cups (300 g)	raisins
1 3/4 cups (150 g)	almonds, peeled and ground
1/2 cup (70 g)	candied lemon peel
1 cup (120 g)	candied orange peel
	Zest of 1 lemon
3	egg yolks
1 tsp	cinnamon, ground
1/2 tsp	clove, ground
6 tbsp	rum
1 pinch	salt
1 1/2 cup (240 g)	marzipan
	butter for spreading inside
1 1/2 cup (300 g)	clarified butter for spreading on the stollen after baking
2 1/3 (300 g)	powdered sugar mixed with vanilla sugar

Christmas stollen [fruit loaf]

All ingredients should be at room temperature before preparation. Completely dissolve yeast in the lukewarm milk and mix in 1/2 tsp granulated sugar and 2 3/4 cups (250 g) of flour. Dust with flour. Cover the sponge and let it rise in a warm place for 30 minutes.

Mix together butter, powdered sugar, a pinch of salt, the rest of the flour, egg yolks, almonds, cinnamon, and clove powder. Blend into sponge until the dough is no longer sticky (about 10 minutes). If the dough gets too firm, add some lukewarm milk.

Mix raisins, finely chopped candied lemon peel and candied orange peel with the rum. Now work the fruit into the batter and let rise for another 30 minutes.

Divide the dough into 4 parts and roll out each part into a thick oval. Use the rolling pin to make a depression down the middle. Form 1/4 cup (60 g) of the marzipan into a log a bit shorter than the dough. Spread some melted butter on the dough, place the marzipan log in the depression and fold the sides over, covering it completely. This gives the stollen its characteristic shape.

Place stollen on a cookie sheet covered with parchment paper and let them rise again. Bake in a preheated oven at 300°F (150°C) for about 50 minutes. After baking, immediately soak in plenty of melted clarified butter and roll in the mixture of powdered and vanilla sugar. Then dust with powdered sugar.

Gingerbread (Lebkuchen)

Mix flour, sugar, baking soda, gingerbread spices, and lemon peel well. Knead into a smooth dough with the eggs and liquid honey. Leave to rest for half an hour.

Preheat oven to 320°F (160°C). Cover cookie sheet with parchment paper. Roll out gingerbread dough so that it is about 1/4 inch thick and cut out the desired forms. Bake for about 20 minutes. After baking, spread 'icing' on them (see Linzer Torte, page 86) or decorate the gingerbread in some other way.

1 1/3 cup (300 g)	rye flour
1 cup (200 g)	raw cane sugar
2	eggs
2 tbsp	honey
1 tsp	baking soda
	grated lemon peel from 1/2 lemon
1 tbsp (15 g)	gingerbread spices or a mixture of ground cinnamon, allspice, nutmeg, cardamom, and cloves

Chocolate dollars

Beat egg whites until stiff. Gradually mix in sugar and vanilla sugar. Fold in chocolate and nuts and stir until the mixture can be piped.

Fill mixture into piping bag with a smooth tip and pipe dollars on a cookie sheet covered with parchment paper. Sprinkle with some powdered sugar and bake in a preheated oven at 320°F (160°C) for about 15–20 minutes. The cookies can be iced with a chocolate icing and decorated with almond slivers or chocolate shavings.

2	egg whites
3/4 cup (140 g)	granulated sugar
2 tsp	vanilla sugar
1 cup (100 g)	chocolate, ground
1 1/2 cup (150 g)	nuts, freshly ground

Vanilla crescents

Use fingertips to work together butter and powdered sugar well on a board. Mix in flour, almonds, and vanilla seeds. Quickly knead to form a smooth dough. If the dough is too dry, it needs some whipping cream. Cover dough with plastic wrap and leave to rest in the refrigerator for about 1 hour.

Form dough into logs. Cut off small pieces and shape individual little crescents by hand. Place on a cookie sheet covered with parchment paper and bake in preheated oven at 350°F (180°C) for about 10 minutes. Roll warm crescents in the sugar-vanilla mixture.

1 cup (200 g)	butter
1/2 cup (70 g)	powdered sugar
2 1/3 cup (280 g)	flour
1 cup (90 g)	almonds, peeled and ground
2	vanilla pods, scraped
	powdered sugar, vanilla sugar, and some granulated sugar for rolling
	some whipping cream

1 3/4 cup (240 g) powdered sugar
2 1/2 cup (240 g) nuts (hazel nuts
and/or walnuts),
ground
2 egg whites, beaten
stiff with a pinch
of salt
2 tbsp pastry flour
1 pinch of cinnamon

Icing
1 egg white
1 cup (130 g) powdered sugar
juice of 1/2 lemon

The consistency of the icing can be
changed by adding powdered sugar
to taste.

2 egg whites
2/3 cup (140 g) granulated sugar
1 cup (140 g) dates, finely chopped
1 1/2 cup (140 g) almonds, ground
wafers (little round
circles, rice paper
rounds can also be used)

Nut macaroons

Mix powdered sugar, nuts, flour, and cinnamon in a bowl. Gradually work in the beaten egg white until it becomes a smooth mixture. Fill the mixture into a piping bag with a medium-sized, smooth tip and pipe macaroons onto a cookie sheet covered with parchment paper. Now spread the icing onto the nut macaroons and press a whole hazelnut into the center of each one.

It's best to let the cookies dry overnight. Then bake them in a preheated oven, which should be left open slightly, at 320°F (160°C) for about 12–14 minutes.

You can also spread blackberry or raspberry jam spread on the bottom of the nut cookies and put two together. However, it is advisable to make the macaroons somewhat smaller for this variation.

Date kisses

Whisk egg whites until stiff and slowly add the sugar. Fold almonds and dates into mixture. Use a teaspoon to place small heaps on the wafers.

Bake in preheated oven at 340°F (170°C) for about 15 minutes, then turn off heat and let them dry for another 15–20 minutes with an open oven door.

'... highly recommended in every respect'

Johanna takes leave with a heavy heart

The most alert among the Trapp children had perhaps already noticed that Hannerl sometimes appeared to be far away in her thoughts. Not that this had affected the quality of the food, yet she was sometimes seen in a corner of the kitchen writing diligently and then hastily taking an envelope to the post office in the afternoon. The yearned-for response would arrive a few days later. She bashfully concealed the letter with its strikingly beautiful handwriting in her apron. Had the cherry sprigs she watered on Saint Barbara's day actually blossomed? In any case, Johanna Raudaschl took heart around Christmas 1931 and told Baroness Maria Augusta von Trapp that she planned to give up her position as cook in order to return home to Lake Attersee – and to get married.

My grandmother maintained a discreet silence throughout her life as to how she met her future husband Johann Georg Hemetsberger, presumably at the beginning of the 1920s. There is much reason to believe that she had first encountered the respected owner of the hereditary farm – the Niedermayrhof, mentioned in

documents as early as 1347 – and proprietor of the local sawmill, during her apprenticeship at the Wiesinger. Before entering into a commitment, however, she had considered it important to still learn a great deal and see something of the world, which for her at the time was the size of the Salzkammergut region. She also wanted to be faithful to her good resolutions, always be wary of her heart, and not fall in love before she could cook.

All her dreams, hopes, and plans had been fulfilled. Despite the poor conditions at the start of her life, she had succeeded in making something of herself, gathering experience, and learning a profession like she had always desired. The months in the Trapp household were her 'final qualification', both the conclusion and culmination of her years of apprenticeship in various places. It was a time that was to leave its mark forever. But now Johanna was ready to settle down and create a new life for herself at the side of the man she loved. Sad and sorry as the Trapp family was to lose such a treasure and miss out on Johanna Raudaschl's culinary resourcefulness, they nevertheless did not want to stand in the way of her happiness. As a sign of gratitude and recognition, Baroness Maria Augusta von Trapp eventually added one of her own favorite dishes to Johanna's considerable recipe collection, the legendary 'Knörpeltorte'. Although quite a challenging work of art, when it turns out well it is a unique-looking and, above all, delicious dessert.

The snow in Salzburg was six feet high. It was to be a long cold winter, worse than any that even the oldest people could remember. On January 2, 1932, a frosty clear day, the Trapp family released Johanna Raudaschl from her position. The Baroness wrote her a good letter of reference and confirmed in writing that she could highly recommend her in every respect.

I hereby confirm that Johanna Raudaschl was employed by me as a cook from 6/6/1931 to 1/1/1932. She is an excellent cook of both simple and fine cuisine, is very skillful, quiet, and modest and is to be highly recommended in every respect.

They all wished her good luck and God's blessing for her future. Johanna could well use the good luck and the blessing. Although she was happy to receive the excellent letter of reference and the recommendation, they never fulfilled their purpose. After all, Johanna did not want to accept any further positions. In view of her future task as a farmer's wife on the hereditary farm, she merely attended a dairy course in order to become familiar with the tasks that had not been part of her training up to that time. A certificate showing that Johanna Raudaschl had earned a clear 'excellent' in the fields of 'Milking and Livestock Care' and 'Dairy Processing and Home Economics' but only a 'Commendable' in 'Cow and Pig Breeding' proved that she was more interested in practical work than in theoretical knowledge.

So Johanna was now optimally equipped to tie the knot with Georg Hemetsberger on May 15, 1933. She had always been an early riser, thus the wedding took place just after sunrise at six a.m. in the parish church of Nussdorf. It was a moving celebration, the happiest day in Johanna's life, although some may have seen it differently. Years later, village gossip was still all about the fact that HE, one of the most eligible bachelors in Nussdorf had not married a farmer's daughter worthy of him, but decided on an 'outsider', and at that, one born out of wedlock. Johanna did not deserve Georg, they said, because there had been other girls of suitable age in the village who were all interested in marrying the wealthy Hemetsberger.

Upright and self-confident, Johanna took the path that seemed right to her, even if it was at times somewhat removed from the village conventions. Even in her later years, it had never been her desire to become one of the traditional 'golden headdress' women whose caps are still passed down from generation to generation, from mother to daughter. She lived her life in her own way and was faithful to the principle of 'recognizing the will of God and acting in accordance with it' – just like Baroness Maria Augusta von Trapp had encouraged her to do when they parted.

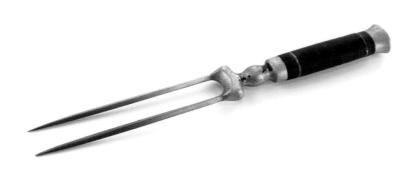

Knörpel

2 3/4 cup (280g)	flour
1/2 tsp	baking powder
1 cup (140g)	powdered sugar
4	egg yolks
1	egg
1 tbsp	rum
	clarified butter

Binding mixture

1 cup (140g)	almonds, flaked
1/2 cup (70g)	candied lemon peel, diced
1/2 cup (70g)	candied orange peel, diced
	Zest of 1/2 lemon
1 tsp	cinnamon
1 tsp	cloves, powdered
2 1/2 cup (500g)	granulated sugar
2 tbsp (15ml)	rose water
2/3 cup (150ml)	water
1 tsp	rum

This recipe is for one large tart or ten small individual tarts.

Knörpeltorte
(Tart Recipe from
Baroness Maria Augusta von Trapp)

To make the knörpel, knead flour, baking powder, sugar, egg yolks, egg, and rum into a firm dough. Shape logs the size of a pencil on a floured surface and cut off pieces about 1/3 inch (1 cm) long. Deep-fry them in batches in the clarified butter. The knörpel more than double in size when deep-fried.

Remove knörpel with slotted spoon and drain on a paper towel.

Heat sugar, rose water, water, and rum in a large pot on the stove. Add almonds, candied lemon peel, candied orange peel, lemon zests, cinnamon, powdered cloves, and – finally – the knörpel. Let it warm well. Cover a counter with parchment paper and press the mixture into the little tartlet pans, cover with a board, and place a heavy weight on top. Put in a cold place and remove from the form the next day. The knörpel tartlets will keep for several weeks.

Memories linger on

Staying in touch

Even after her wedding, my grandmother stayed in touch with Baroness Maria Augusta von Trapp. So she discovered in 1934 – just as Johanna had given birth to her first son Georg – that the family had plunged into a major personal crisis through the bankruptcy of the Lammer bank in the town of Zell am See. All of their assets were lost from one day to the next. The staff, which also included Johanna's successor as cook, had to be dismissed. With much faith in God, they had initially attempted to make financial ends meet by renting out rooms. For Johanna, it was an almost inconceivable thought that the 'masters' had moved up into the servants' quarters where she had once lived while they rented their own rooms to strangers. It was easier for her to imagine that the wonderful singing of the children would secure their future livelihood. While the Trapp Chamber Choir celebrated one success after the other under the direction of the private chaplain Monsignor Dr. Franz Wasner including first prize in the Folksong Competition at the Salzburg Festival, Johanna had more children as

she had always wanted: her son Karl was born in 1935, a daughter – who was to be called Johanna again – followed in 1937, and, the youngest son Manfred finally in 1943.

When the Trapp Family had to leave Austria in 1938 on the run from the Nazis and immigrated to America, contact broke off for a while. Perhaps the Trapps sometimes wondered what had become of the modest young woman from back then? How had she survived the difficult times during the war? It may have been a comforting thought to them that Johanna and her loved ones at least never had to suffer from hunger because of her talent for making something out of almost nothing.

Even in her later years, Johanna passionately followed the musical career of the family – which was soon famous throughout the world –, read the books by Maria Augusta von Trapp, and saved all the reports about the choir that appeared in the local newspapers. For a while she even received the group letters that the Baroness von Trapp wrote to her 'Dear Friends' in the old homeland and in which she shared her family and concert life. There was naturally great sadness because of the Baron's death in May 1947. However, there was also good news since tours took the group, now called the Trapp Family Singers, around the world – from South America to Oceania to Australia. After the Second World War, Maria Augusta von Trapp organized a highly respected relief campaign and collected clothing and food after the concerts. She was able to send tens of thousands of these CARE packages to friends and relatives in Austria, for which the Baroness received awards including the Golden Decoration for Services to the Republic of Austria in 1957 and the Austrian Cross of Honor for Science and Art first Class in 1967.

In 1950, the singing Trapp Family performed at the Festival in Salzburg. Johanna was somewhat troubled that she had never succeeded in all the years to see this concert or any of the approximately 2,000 concerts given by the choir before it disbanded in 1956. On the other hand, SHE had been allowed to experience their beginnings up close and had fond memories of companionable evenings with them making music together at home.

In her Christmas letter of 1977, Maria Augusta dedicated the picture and text to the memory of her husband as she wrote: 'He was the most famous navy hero of Austria back then, who had accomplished unbelievable things with his tiny submarine. He showed his true heroic nature during the second half of his life when he chose to emigrate with his large family instead of conforming with Hitler's false philosophy. Now he rests under the trees of our little cemetery behind the house. From his heavenly bridge, the Captain has already victoriously steered the little ship with his family through many storms and – so we hope – will one day guide it into the harbor of eternity.'

Johanna had always been a passionate moviegoer. She had hardly permitted herself any other pleasures during her time in Salzburg. So the last two pages of the little notebook that she kept 1931 were full of cinema reviews such as: 'Zentral Kino [movie theater]: *Die Förster Christl* – beautiful!,' 'Mirabell Kino: *3 lustige Musikanten* – funny!,' or 'Lifka: *Schwebende Jungfrau* – hilarious!' She would never have dreamed that a film would be shown in 1956 – the German production of *The Trapp Family* – that was based on a true story in which she herself had been involved. Neither would she have missed a film made two years later in 1958, *The Trapp Family in America* with Ruth Leuwerick, Hans Holt, and Josef Meinrad in the leading roles. On the other hand, she only knew by hearsay about the musical that came later – *The Sound of Music* – and the Hollywood film with the same title. Hugely popular as its was and still is throughout Britain and North America, in Salzburg the 1965 film with Julie Andrews and Christopher Plummer was removed from the program after just a few days.

Memories also lingered on the other side of the Atlantic, in Stowe, Vermont, where the Trapp Family had finally settled down and assumed American citizenship. 'Memories of the homeland and the desire to see it again.' was a

Liebe Freunde!

Dieses Bild ist jetzt 50 Jahre alt—wir waren damals ganz jung verheiratet. Ich habe es für meine heurige Weihnachtskarte gewählt, um das Andenken an meinen Mann, Kapitän Georg von Trapp, wieder aufleben zu lassen. Er war ja damals der berühmteste Marineheld Österreichs, der mit seinem winzigen U-Boot unglaubliches vollbracht hat.

Seine wahre Heldennatur hat sich aber dann in der zweiten Hälfte seines Lebens gezeigt, als er lieber mit seiner grossen Familie auswanderte, als sich der falschen Philosophie Hitler's anzuschliessen.

Jetzt ruht er unter den Bäumen unseres kleinen Friedhofs hinter dem Haus. Aber von seiner himmlischen Kommandobrücke aus hat der Kapitän das Schifflein seiner Familie schon durch viele Stürme siegreih gelenkt und wird es—so hoffen wir—einst in den Hafen der Ewigkeit führen.

Ich hatte noch ein anderes Jubiläum zu feiern in diesem vergangenen Jahr: meine 55 jährige Maturafeier. Von einer Klasse von 24 Kameradinnen sind 15 noch am Leben und 10 davon haben sich in Wien getroffen Da sind wir "älteren Damen," lauter Grossmütter, beisammen gesessen und haben einander erzählt; es ist ja soviel passiert in dieser Zeit—in der Welt und in unserem Leben.

Und dann sind noch Nachrichten von der Familie zu berichten, Drei Enkelinnen haben geheiratet:

Rupert's älteste Tochter, Monika
Lorli's (Mrs. Hugh Campbell's) zweite Tochter, Peggy
Werner's älteste Tochter, Barbara
Und im Oktober hat Tobi (Werner's dritter Sohn) und seine Frau Sally eine kleine Emilie Sarah bekommen, mein achtes Urenkelkind.

Die aufregendste Neuigkeit aber ist momentan, dass unser Haus, die Trapp Family Lodge, erneuert und vergrössert werden soll, Tische sind bedeckt mit grossen Plänen, A, B, C, dann wieder zurück zu A. Jetzt hoffe ich nur, dass wir rechtzeitig mit "dem" Plan fertig werden, damit ich euch im nächsten Weihnachtsbrief ein Bild von der neuen "Trapp Family Lodge" zeigen kann.

Es grüsst von Herzen

Eure.

Maria von Trapp

Maria and Georg Ritter von Trapp usually sent their greetings to friends every year with a printed Christmas letter for the holidays.

touching excerpt of the December 1964 letter from Maria Augusta von Trapp: 'As we drove by on the autobahn outside of Salzburg and for the first time again saw the Fortress and the Untersberg, tears came to our eyes [...] Something odd happened in Salzburg. The Hollywood people, who were making a film about the Trapp Family, were just doing their location shots in Salzburg. We very briefly met the producers and the leading actors. When I joked that I would like to walk across the street in front of the camera, they took me literally and Barbara, Rosmarie, and I can be seen in the film as we walk across the Domplatz. In terms of the film, I must admit that I'm still uneasy about it. I have always tried in all possible ways to meet the people in charge because I wanted to explain Captain Trapp – who is not portrayed in a very good way on stage – to them. Unfortunately, this was not possible because they simply were not interested in the truth. They wanted to film their own version, they said. And now we are fearful about what Hollywood will make out of the Trapp Family.'

Unfounded concerns? One of the last of these group letters found in my grandmother's estate, which also had the deathbed picture of Maria Augusta von Trapp from the year 1987, contained these lines: 'As you probably still remember from last year, we were all very worried about what Hollywood would do with us in the film *The Sound of Music*. Thank God that all our fears were unnecessary. The film turned out very beautiful, especially the scenes shot in the vicinity of Salzburg from a helicopter, the magnificent landscape, the alpine pastures with the spring flowers [...] I would like to emphasize here that we had nothing to do whatsoever with the film and were therefore quite surprised by the very dramatic ending. Otherwise, it is really beautiful and has been unbelievably successful with audiences: people see it not just once, but many times, up to twenty, thirty, and even fifty times. Unfortunately, we did not have an attorney when we signed the contract [...]'. And Maria Augusta von Trapp concluded her letter with the words:

'A little more peace and lot less strife,
less envy, more love, for a happier life,
and many more flowers
when we're still above ground,
for they are in vain
when we're under the mound.'

Caroline Kleibel and Irmgard Wöhrl select the ingredients together for The Trapp Cookbook.

Epilogue

The memories of Johanna Raudaschl's life were partially preserved in the form of calendar entries, notes, and marginal comments on the recipes in her cookbooks, as well as in correspondence and fragmentary reminiscences that her family advised her to record in her later years. Many things about her life were only passed on by word of mouth, related especially by her elder son Georg Hemetsberger, who lived in the same household with his mother until she died in 1993. Her daughter, Johanna Wiesinger – Irmgard Wöhrl's mother – and her youngest son, Manfred Hemetsberger, also preserved many of these memories.

Only the various perspectives can result in an overall picture that approaches reality but is never a perfect replica of it. The nature of memories is probably that they are influenced by subjectivity. Stories are never told completely without any gaps. So we cannot make the claim that all of the events described here happened exactly in this way and not differently. At times it appears necessary to just speculate how things might have been, in view of a complete sequence of events based on the sources of contemporary history. In any case, it is certain that the months in the Trapp House had a special meaning for Johanna Raudaschl, who had never before been able to experience such solidarity in a family. And this is true even if – despite all the recognition she received – she was just one of many servants for the members of the Trapp Family. All the more impressive, then, is Maria von Trapp's active support in tracing the course of events. In a long conversation, she showed how touched she was by the accurate and detailed descriptions, and was able to confirm many things from her own point of view.

It was fascinating to interweave the biographies of these two family histories, to let the lives of two strong women – Johanna Raudaschl and the now legendary Baroness Maria Augusta von Trapp – cross in this period and then part again to take different directions. After all, nothing is more exciting than recording and preserving the stories that life writes.

Caroline Kleibel
(Caroline Kleibel has been working as a journalist and biographer over more than 25 years, portraying well-known celebrities' as well as other people's everyday life stories.)

For 1 1/3 gallon (5 liter) starter

60	green, halved nuts (picked around the time of the summer solstice)
1 cup (40g)	cinnamon sticks
1/3 cup (40g)	ginger, sliced
3/4 cup (40g)	cloves, whole
1/2 cup (20g)	absinthe wormwood
1/2 cup (20g)	centaurium
1	vanilla pod
1 1/3 cup (300g)	rock candy
1/3 cup (20g)	gentian root
1 cup (60g)	calamus root
1 cup (60g)	star anise
5 liter	schnapps (fruit schnapps or Slivovitz)
	sugar syrup according to taste

Nut schnapps

Divide all of the spices and nuts (except for the sugar syrup) equally into one or more jars and fill with the schnapps. Close the jars and leave to steep for about 3 months in a sunny place. Then strain through a filter and sweeten with sugar syrup according to taste. Allow to mature for a few more months.

For my grandmother nut schnapps was a remedy for all kinds of stomach upsets. It was also often served just as a pleasant conclusion to a good meal. To your good health!

The authors would like to acknowledge

Johanna Wiesinger
Georg Hemetsberger
Manfred Hemetsberger
Franz Leitner
Elfriede Mayrhofer
Therese und Wolfgang Kleibel
Heiner Kolbe
Ilse Ganahl †
Dorothea Rákóczy †
Beate Haderer
Franz Wendl
Brigitte Gruber

And very special thanks to
Maria von Trapp

Conversion Table

Kitchen Measurements and Weights

1 pinch = about 1–2 g

1 level teaspoon (tsp) =
2 g cinnamon
3 g paprika powder or corn starch
5 g fat, oil, salt, or sugar
5 ccm water

1 level tablespoon (tbsp) =
10 g flour or corn starch
10 g powdered sugar
12 g fat or oil
15 g salt or granulated sugar
15 ccm water
1 shot is equivalent to half a schnapps glass of vinegar, wine, etc.

Liquid Measurements

1 cl (centiliter) = 0.01 l = 10 ccm
1 dl (deciliter) = 0.1 l = 100 ccm
6 tbsp = 0.1 l = 100 ccm
8 tbsp = 0.125 l = 125 ccm

Recommended serving sizes

Meat 150–200 g
Fish 200–250 g (main course)
Fresh vegetables 150–250 g
Legumes 100–125 g
Potatoes 250–300 g
Fruit 100–125 g
Rice 80–100 g (main course)
Soup 2.5 dl (starter), 0.5 l (main course)
Pasta 100–125 g (main course)